JOURNEY TO THE

AN AMAZING STORY OF RISK-TAKING IN BUSINESS AND ADVENTURE

Enda O'Coineen

Ballpoint Press

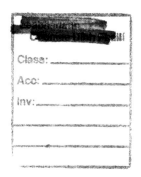

Published in 2019 by Ballpoint Press
4 Wyndham Park, Bray,
Co Wicklow, Republic of Ireland.

Telephone: 00353 86 821 7631
Email: ballpointpress1@gmail.com
Web: www.ballpointpress.ie

ISBN 978-1-9998306-8-7

Book design and production by Joe Coyle Media&Design,
joecoyledesign@gmail.com

Also by the Author:
Kilcullen (Mercier Press, 1977)
The Unsinkable Kilcullen (Bodley Head, 1987)
SAIL Ireland (Kilcullen Press, 1991)
The Unsinkable Entrepreneur (Mercier Press, 2009)

Film Documentaries:
My Own Place (RTÉ, 1980)
Secret Millionaire (RTÉ, 2014)
Journey to the Edge (Business Post Media Group with Esras Productions)

Printed and bound by GraphyCems

Contents

Foreword

Michael D. Higgins
President of Ireland

"Boats are safe in harbour, but that's not what boats are for"
John A Shedd

THE connection between Ireland and the ocean is as old as time itself and the sea has played a fundamental part in our social and economic history. As an island people, our proximity to the sea has historically created a special form of vulnerability to the forces of nature as we have looked outwards and beyond landfall to create a sustainable future from that great natural resource.

Ireland's relationship with the ocean has not of course always been a positive one. In the 19th century it was synonymous with forced emigration on Famine ships, escaping the Great Hunger of the 1840s, with many perishing en route to North America. In the 20th century, many Irish crossed the Irish Sea in search of a more economically and socially fulfilling life. In recent times, the relationship has become positive, thankfully.

Island nations are, of necessity perhaps, outward-looking, interested in the world beyond, in its promises and its dangers, their culture emphasising a warm welcome for a stranger. This value placed on hospitality is understandable, perhaps amongst people who are familiar with setting sail themselves, across oceans to new destinations, of appreciating a welcome where they come ashore.

There is a realisation amongst islanders and seafarers, I believe, from their literature and lived experience that the world is something that is encountered, closer to us than our maps and charts might suggest, that what happens thousands of miles away will have its say much closer to home.

As John Donne most famously put it 400 years ago about one of the regions of our connected world:

"No man is an island,
Entire of itself,
Every man is a piece of the continent,
A part of the main.
if a clod be washed away by the sea, Europe
is the less......."

At the heart of this insight is an understanding of our interdependency that is the very antithesis of any forced exploitative interconnection, historic or contemporary, be it of extractive industries, resources or trade.

Enda O'Coineen's book, *Journey to the Edge*, details a personal journey, a solo circumnavigation across the seas, as well as his competing in the prestigious Vendée Globe. However, the voyage transpired to be more than just a personal adventure; it was a challenge both physically and psychologically, one that tested the human spirit to its limits and revealed the power from within, the fortitude and determination that is inside us all, often untapped.

The voyage evolves into a beautiful obsession, guided only by the goals he sets himself. When O'Coineen did not succeed in sailing around the world at his first attempt due to a broken mast, he honoured his initial goal and succeed on his second attempt.

The book is anything but a dry account of a journey around the world on a yacht; it is a personal and spiritual journey in which O'Coineen draws lessons at the end of each chapter from the various legs of the adventure. Never shy from reflecting on the big existential questions, he offers sage advice from personal experience and reflections in a fast-paced and exciting narrative that is never dull and often thought-provoking.

I congratulate Enda on his voyage of discovery and for the publication of this book which will be of interest not just to lovers of the sea, but to all great adventurers, young and old.

August, 2019

Prologue
The Start

IT was like a massive explosion. There was turbulence, noise; and then it was deathly quiet.

In a matter of a few seconds my whole world had fallen apart.

And with those few moments went my dream of sailing solo around the world.

Or so it seemed. . .

There I was in the vast expanse of the Pacific Ocean, converging on the international dateline, heading for Cape Horn and everything was coming apart in my world — and on my 60-foot yacht.

My boat suddenly went on her side.

Crouched in the cockpit, fighting with the rudder, I remember staring at the wind speed: 20 knots, then 25, then 30, then 35 and it kept rising fast.

Frighteningly fast.

I'd never seen anything like it.

This was my first time to experience wind surging with such dramatic speed and with so little forewarning in that part of the Pacific.

The entire rig went. It blasted over the side. The load was so great the mast couldn't take it any longer.

My whole life raced before my eyes as I scurried instinctively to at least save the boat.

The problem, if that is not too small a word to describe the dire circumstances, was that the stump of the mast was banging and bashing like a loose cannon into the boat.

Left to its own devices, it would almost certainly punch a hole in the hull. So the safest thing to do was to cut it all away.

Not an easy task.

It took 30 minutes of absolute chaos to clear everything. By then, as I surveyed the wreckage of the boat (and my dream) I was totally exhausted, mentally and physically.

There was nothing left to do except cry.

Yes, cry.

For all of my life right up to that moment, my major desire at every level of my being was to complete a solo circumnavigation.

And now all seemed lost.

¶ ¶ ¶ ¶

The happy-go-lucky time that had marked the start of my dream seemed such a long time ago.

It had begun with an impulse.

I had bought the boat at one in the morning for a seven-figure sum exactly 24 months previously.

Yes, it was a big risk. But that's what I do.

I take risks.

Indeed, this is a story of Risk: its evolution and its understanding.

I've been taking risks all my life. But for the purposes of this adventure I suppose I really committed to Risk shortly after a New Year's party.

I'd called the owner of the yacht at 1am and did the deal there and then and bought the boat.

In doing so, my resolution crystallised. It was to sail solo around the world and fulfil a lifelong dream.

It would not just be an attempt at circumnavigation. I also set out to qualify and compete in what is regarded as the toughest sporting event there is: The Vendée Globe.

I'll admit now that in the cold light of day, I should never have made the decision to buy the yacht on the spur of the moment.

But there was a certain euphoria starting the New Year and I felt my time had come.

I was sober; my wife Nicola spurred me on by saying: "Go for it."

I did.

And what transpired was to be much more than just sailing, much more than an autobiographical journey. It was to give me the ultimate challenges on so many levels — both physically and psychologically — and in some ways, mirror my life in business, risk, politics, love, sport, family and charity where, I think it is fair to say, I have shown a stubborn determination and a desire to succeed at all costs — well, almost.

The idea, the dream, the urge, the drive (call it what you will) had been in my mind and my heart for a long time. Yet it really only began to take real shape on a whim. A whim that compelled me to buy the boat in the middle of the night. Just like that.

Chapter 1

Understanding
The Journey

IT is always difficult to know where something starts, to pinpoint where the idea, the challenge first bites. All my life I've wanted to do things. Some seem to have been with me forever. Others just grew and grew until they took hold of me and sparked me into action.

All I know is that I became addicted to doing things, to wanting to test myself against the toughest and the best.

And they don't come much tougher, or better, than sailing around the world on your own.

The idea, the dream, the urge, the drive (call it what you will) had been in my mind and my heart for a long time.

Yet it really only began to take real shape on a whim.

A whim that compelled me to buy the boat in the middle of the night. Just like that.

An impulse.

As if something was directing me.

So I'll nail that as the starting point of my great adventure.

The upshot of my impulsive, if costly, decision to buy the yacht was to give me an immediate and sharp focus on how to go about fulfilling my dream of sailing solo around the world. Of course I had been thinking about doing it for some time.

But would I have made such a decision in the cold light of day?

No.

I was euphoric, you see. I often get that way around New Year.

And on that occasion I just felt my time had come.

The thing was, I had recently concluded a good business deal, so I felt I could afford to take the risk.

There's that word you are going to hear from me many times. Risk.

It is the key concept at the centre of my journey.

It shaped what I did, and when and how.

People thought I was mad to undertake such an adventure.

And maybe I was.

Maybe I still am.

But I was prepared to take the risks. Taking a risk not only brings satisfaction at braving the odds. It also helps search for, and ponder on, a greater understanding of what this life is all about. It breeds acceptance that in real, proper life, there can be no safety net.

It's all or nothing for me anyway.

So while, on one level, this is a story about circumnavigating the world, it is also more intricate, complicated and profound than that daunting task on its own.

I hope you will agree with me on that by the time you've finished reading this.

I would contend that its ramifications reach far beyond the autobiographical detail and challenges of an ocean voyage.

¶ ¶ ¶ ¶

Risk-taking flows through my life: business, politics, love, sport, family and charity. It's what I do; what I am.

For all that, I know and lament the fact that this book is written against the emergence of an increasingly 'risk-averse' society where perspective is so often lost.

I strongly believe that our freedom as individuals in society is slowly eroding. We want the comfort of certainty and are prepared to forgo a lot for that security of tenure.

Deciding to circumnavigate the world on my own was perhaps the most emphatic, public and personal challenge I'd undertaken.

But be sure of one thing: it loudly proclaimed my desire to swim against the tide.

That is a trait of mine and explains why this voyage is all about stubborn determination, refusal to give up, of challenging the odds, of wanting to succeed at all cost. Well, almost all.

LESSONS FROM CHAPTER 1

- If you think too much about doing something new or different, you might never do it.
- Be really careful about what New Year Resolutions you make. It's easy to talk but 'doing it' is another matter altogether.
- We all need to think in 'contrarian' ways from time to time.

Imagine, one of the largest ships in the world had altered course, turned around and was trying to save me. And I was spurning their kind offer.

Chapter 2
Please Don't Save Me

THERE I was, all alone on board my 60-foot thoroughbred ocean racing yacht after leaving Cape Horn astern.

All of a sudden this massive cruise liner hovered over me. The crew wanted to rescue me. They thought I was in trouble — I was somewhere between the remote Falkland Islands and Tierra del Fuego, Chile.

But nothing could be further from the truth: I was solely focussed on completing my solo circumnavigation.

Much to their surprise, no doubt, I told them I had no desire to be rescued.

Imagine — one of the largest ships in the world had altered course, turned around and was trying to save me. And I was spurning their kind offer.

You see, I had been almost a month at sea at that stage and it was my first encounter with another vessel since departing New Zealand.

To be 'rescued' was not an option. Not after I'd sailed through the most remote oceans in the world and rounded the notorious Cape Horn (its reputation, for reasons I will explain later, is well deserved).

It was evening. Life was good. Ahead lay the prospect of another beautiful sunset on my voyage. The wind was moderate and a gentle sea rolled — though the weather map said it might build a little.

Preparing to head into the darkness, I was changing headsails and putting a reef in when, in the distance I saw a ship pass. She was headed north.

Her name was, I think, The Island Princess, out of Bermuda, which (I guessed) had followed me around Cape Horn by some distance.

She first went past. I noticed her and that was it.

Or so I thought.

Sometime later, while below deck, I heard a loud horn hoot. Alarmed, I looked up to see this massive ship hovering above my yacht in the light of the evening as the sun set on the south Atlantic.

Obviously the ship I had seen in the distance had come back. That constituted a massive exercise for a vessel of its size: all for little old me. Thinking I was in trouble, they were almost on top of my yacht.

I stared at the gallery of crew and passengers lined up on their starboard side. We were almost within earshot. It was bizarre.

As you probably know, these ships are floating cities; massive vacuum cleaners that suck up huge quantities of money. The industry has enjoyed enormous growth; ships ply their global trade virtually non-stop.

For those who can afford them, they are islands in the sea disconnected from the real world. They facilitate a fantasy, a retreat into a floating delusional world of night clubs, casinos, duty free shops, restaurants, spas, wellness centres and much more. Good luck to them and the ATM machines they represent.

Tragically, however, the tourism dollar stays with the ships while revenue for the local communities visited is just 'breadcrumbs'. Indeed, visiting some small island countries — where the turnover of one ship would likely be bigger than their gross income — they do a lot of damage. Those on board are totally disconnected from where they visit.

I have seen this at play in places such as Haiti or St Lucia in the Caribbean. Life on a cruiser is not really of the ocean, the environment or being close to nature. It's a world of rampant consumerism.

But, I digress. Back to the unwanted 'rescue' attempt.

Mesmerised by the sight of that towering ship, I reacted quickly — from fear and excitement. It was an emotional rush after being alone for so long, and my mind raced. I grabbed the handheld VHF and called the ship on channel 16 — the international emergency calling channel.

Up to then, being in such a remote location, I'd had no radio on, nor did I need it. Swiftly the ship's bridge responded:

"Is all well on board sir?"

"Actually I'm fine," I said. "I really appreciate your attention and turning around but I do not need help."

I was as apologetic as possible and added that I did not wish to cause any inconvenience. I told them I would most certainly have called, or sent a flare, if I had been in trouble when they passed earlier.

With everything from satellite phones, emergency flares, two life rafts, survival rations and a medical kit sufficient to run a small hospital with, I was just fine.

It emerged from further conversation with the ship's bridge that sighting me had sparked quite a deal of excitement on board. Apparently, after some tourists had spotted the boat, one extremely concerned man, God bless him, led a delegation to the bridge. They were convinced they had seen someone in trouble and asked that the captain go back. The captain felt obliged to do so.

Before parting with them, I also had friendly chat with the ship's radio operator. I told him that my destination was France. He said he would be in Paris on April 9th so I invited him for a drink at O'Sullivan's Irish Pub. I guessed the owner, Tom St John, would oblige him with a pint. To this day I'm curious to know if he showed up.

LESSONS FROM CHAPTER 2

↗ Ocean life on board cruise liners is very different to that of a solo sailor.

↗ You may not want or need help, but other people might want to help. So, even in remote locations, leave your radio on.

↗ Don't try to save those who do not wish to be rescued.

Chapter 3

What Is It About New Year's Day?

THERE is something about New Year's Day — for me anyway.
It was at 1am, New Year's Day 2015 that this adventure started with the phone call to buy the boat.

I committed to writing this book on January 1st 2018.

And on New Year's Day 2017, within hours of resolving to take less risks with my life, I was shipwrecked and almost died.

I will return in greater detail to that January 2017 disaster, but let me start as my second-attempt circumnavigation adventure is taking shape.

I still picture my 12-year-old son, Cormac, sitting beside me on the plane to New Zealand, not really sure what his dad is up to. He is along for the ride and the send-off of what promises to be a wonderful expedition for us all as I get ready to complete my circumnavigation of New Zealand for starters.

We are 35,000 feet above Australia on the way to the world of Kiwis.

Soon I will be setting sail, from where I was forced to leave off: to sail alone back to 'unofficially finish' the Vendée Global Race. It has been a long haul back to being able to do so, after suffering the heartbreak of having my first attempt smashed and battered by forces far greater than most people can imagine.

Some would call it tempting fate heading off over the massive Pacific and around Cape Horn.

Others would say I was stone mad.

But stones sink and to succeed and survive it is necessary to be distressingly sane and organised.

"If you're living on the edge, you are taking up too much space," as Winston Churchill said.

This narrative is about adventure and risk and sometimes going beyond the edge. But it is all bundled in with the more mundane standard package of New Year resolutions. They include the regulars, such as getting fitter, eating better, making business plans, spending more time with loved ones and putting something back to make the world a better place.

But now, as each New Year comes around, age prods with a greater sense of urgency. For me it is the polar opposite to the Spanish word 'mañana'.

I also think of the famous quip by Patrick Kavanagh to BBC interviewer David Dimbleby who, in an aristocratic condescending accent, asked: "Now sir, what was your equivalent word (to manana) in the Gaelic language?"

The reply was: "We have no word that conveys the same sense of urgency."

I like to take from the words of Samuel Beckett:
"Perhaps my best years are gone...
but I wouldn't want them back.
Not with the fire in me now"

These are words that help sum up what I believe to be drive and passion. As I get older I have fewer years to pack it all in. They say guys my age shouldn't do stuff like this. That is crock.

But it does bring me to the subject of Why.

Why do we do things?

Why am I setting out?

Why such risk?

It's a complex concoction of need, hunger, drive, ambition, vanity and good old-fashioned fear (I will get to that later).

Just as fear is the flipside of need, risk is the flipside of reward and hate can tragically be the flipside of love.

I would contend that civilisation, as we know it, is being driven to the edge and as members of a now-global society we are becoming increasingly polarised. Could it be that clever computer algorithms are accelerating this process through technology and the internet?

Some suggest that my last book, *The Unsinkable Entrepreneur* had an error in the title which perhaps should have read "Unthinkable".

Perhaps.

Tracing three stages in life it picked up on me being:

▶ A chancer;

▶ An entrepreneur;

▶ A philanthropist.

Now I have arrived at that 'perfect' Fourth Stage.

It comes after almost getting everything right, but not perfectly right.

Now I have found 'perfection'. A perfect eejit, more like, but if I don't do what I want to do now I may never get another chance. Maybe that is something I share with many in my age group. It came as a bit of a shock to recently find that the highest number of successful entrepreneurs were people in the 55-65 year bracket.

The entrepreneurial urge not only impacts on business at this age: it also positively affects people founding charities and social organisations.

I always thought that being an entrepreneur and taking risk was a young person's game. It is almost the opposite.

There is, indeed, wisdom in age.

When people reach maturity they are often at the 'empty nester' stage. Their living costs are lower; the mortgage is most likely paid for.

In short they are — or should be — ready to go and live on the edge for a while and take lots more risk, if only to fight the rules, regulations, controls and insurance which can stifle initiative and make life increasingly dreary and adventure-less.

I believe we are losing our freedom in a slow but creepy way.

Living on the edge and pushing the boundaries does not necessarily involve taking more risk. Essentially to go out front you have to have balls (or to be politically correct) and/or ovaries.

People say: "That fella is totally mad."

Perhaps. I am not the best judge.

From my perspective, the reality is that I might have had a happier and less stressful existence if I was simply 'mad'. In fact 'mad' people can get away with much more than most of those considered sane.

The reality is also you have to be completely sane to undertake the adventures I have encountered, or start charities, build a business enterprise or stand up to establishments.

To run a 60-foot ocean racing boat alone you need to be structured, disciplined, organised and focused. There is no place for madness.

¶ ¶ ¶ ¶

When I was 21, I'd crossed the Atlantic from America to Ireland in a 16-foot inflatable dinghy. It was an incredible adventure. They said I was completely mad. The fact it was an experimental sailing life raft I had developed was completely lost on them.

Then 40 years later (back to January 1st 2017 — there is no escaping it), I had just come through almost two months alone at sea, several bad storms in the Indian Ocean and a knockdown (my 60 footer went on its side, half way to being upside-down).

As it happened I was just over half-way around the world in the Vendée Globe single-handed non-stop around the world race which had started from Les Sables d'Olonne in France.

And now, I have just celebrated the New Year at 35,000 feet en route back to New Zealand to go to sea yet again.

It is to finish what I set out to do and sail singlehanded around the world, originally non-stop and now with 'one-stop'.

The 'one-stop' involves a circumnavigation of New Zealand with more than 3,000 miles of amazing, treacherous and beautiful coastline.

As a diversion it was to be a good training ground for my boat and body as I strove to become the first Irishman to circumnavigate the country. I cannot find a record of any other who has done so.

Such is my West of Ireland outlook that for much of my life I have been a contrarian, mould-breaker and the one most likely to argue that black was white.

My new journey was another opportunity to reflect, stand back and try to make sense of things. Even more importantly: what can we — you and I — learn from my adventures and risk-taking as a microcosm of society itself?

As I begin here, seated on a jet, who knows what lies ahead? Cormac, with his 'hoodie' is fast asleep in a world of his own. He has leave from school and has come to see me off.

He is the youngest of my four offspring. The others are Saoirse, Aisling and Roisin (who has made me a grandfather twice over with Arthur and Feile).

I'm still not sure I am even suitable, or ready, to be a parent, never mind a grandparent! Feile was born around the same time I sailed alone across the Equator while moving into the South Atlantic.

But my offspring are growing into a society that is increasingly imploding on itself with less room or place for people on the edge. We are all converging towards the norm.

Yet I have to ask: Was I taking too much risk and stretching the boundaries too far?

Looking back to 1st January 2017, I had clearly decided that I was. Enough was enough.

I felt that so strongly that at one stage I had determined to brief my solicitor to draft a document which I would sign when rational. Essentially it was that, should I decide to push the boundaries again, he or my family could produce the document and stop me from doing it, whatever 'it' might be.

It was only a few hours later on New Year's Day 2017 — after making my firm new resolution — that the mast of my 60-foot ocean racing machine went crashing over the side in big seas.

It was caused by self-steering problems, which I thought I'd solved, and a massive, unexpected squall.

My pride and joy, two years of preparation, aspirations and support of others, were shattered.

My world fell apart.

Or did it?

Well it did and it didn't. That's where we have to expect the unexpected.

That horrendous jolt of reality made me think a lot. It made me think how as a modern society, more than 99.9 percent of the worry, resource, cost and stress goes into solving risks of fewer than 0.1 percent.

Have we lost the plot? Are we becoming a nanny state where individuality, freedom, personality, initiative and all the human traits that make us what we have become are being eroded? Slowly, perhaps, but eroded nonetheless, I believe.

Surely we have the ability and right to choose and decide our own acceptable level of risk rather than have it imposed on us?

I remember, from way back, having to sneak out to sea as I began my first singlehanded voyage across the North Atlantic from America to Europe. That was to dodge the US Coast Guard. It wasn't so much that they cared about me, or were afraid I'd drown. It's just they feared the US taxpayer might have to foot the bill for a massive search-and-rescue operation if I were lost at sea.

But back to New Year's Day 2017 and the mast of my yacht crashing over the side.

As you can imagine it was a horrific time.

But I consoled myself with the fact I had enough food for another two months, and as I'd cut all the mast and rig away, there was no fear the boat would be holed. Even my sat phone was working. Sure what about it if I was deep in the southern ocean and the nearest boat — or fellow member of the human race — was 180 miles away?

I keep mentioning that fateful part of the voyage not merely because of the massive setback it represented. Parallel with the overwhelming emotions, my predicament made me rethink the entire subject of risk, society and what's it all about?

I asked myself: can we learn from this?

I delve more deeply into these questions later. So take your chance, come aboard, and risk learning something.

LESSON FROM CHAPTER 3

- ↗ I always thought that being an entrepreneur and taking risk was a young person's game. It is almost the opposite.
- ↗ Calling something or somebody 'mad' is a cop out. We are insulting ourselves by effectively declaring that something out of the ordinary is something we do not understand.

For it to be a success, experience had taught me I'd have to practise, practise and practise, and get plenty of time on the water. For years I was in awe of these amazing boats; the skills required and the ability of those who sailed them.

Chapter 4
Getting Started

I WAS mad keen to get going on my first attempt to circumnavigate the globe. But it was April before I was finally ready to sail on our maiden voyage.

Don't forget I had bought the boat on New Year's Day.

And preparations involved a survey, detailed preparation, a mini fit-out and several journeys to Southampton where she was berthed.

Mike Golding, the seller, was gracious during the hand-over, including as much knowledge from several circumnavigations as I could data-mine from him.

A legend in British Ocean sailing and adventure, Mike started life as a fireman but eventually came to prominence in the Clipper around the World Race — and then the Vendée Globe.

It was incredibly exciting to be at the Ground Zero of my dream and to get things moving. The boat was in brilliant shape. I determined to get going, learn, learn and learn... and sail to the Canary Islands for Easter.

More specifically I also wanted to get to Lanzarote and Puerto Calero (an ideal deep-water base and training ground).

For it to be a success, experience had taught me I'd have to practise, practise and practise — and get plenty of time on the water. For years I was in awe of these amazing boats; the skills required and the ability of those who sailed them.

My reality was being an older guy and folk of my age don't normally do things like that. It was for the younger, more athletic people.

Anyway, like knowing a man who knew a man who knew a man who ate an elephant (he achieved his goal by eating a little bit at a time) this was my learning and preparation strategy.

There were four of us setting out.

Two younger professional sailors were being paid, yet when it came to the wire they didn't want to go. They were afraid — but wouldn't admit it — so they were finding reasons not to go after doing a good job preparing the boat. It was also early season and cold. And they were rightly nervous about heading straight off-shore to the Canaries.

The other crew man was Joe the engineer — the wonderful son of my wife, Nicola. He was 18 and, if the truth be known, he did not know any better. He was all the better for that. Not knowing what he did not know was a great thing — at least that's how I saw it. Mind you, had Nicola fully realised the risk, she might have stopped him.

I was really comfortable. The other guys were much more nervous. Sometimes you're better not knowing.

I was brimming with anticipation. It was the start of a dream coming true.

Sailing from Southampton, up the Solent leaving the Isle of Wight to port, we went with the tide on a cold spring day. We quickly got going down the Channel and turned the corner at Ushant — around the north west corner of France and southwards to the prospect of warmer weather each day.

We ticked off the distance, one sea mile at a time.

Past Cape Finisterre, off the north-west coast of Spain. The shipping lanes in the black of night were intimidating, but I was happy and we all gradually got more comfortable with the boat — which is a truly intricate piece of equipment. With two hydro-generators, two desalination plants, 10 water ballast tanks, a keel that moved, complex rigging, dagger boards, zillions of control lines and complex electronics, two self-steering systems, computers and satellite equipment, there was a lot to learn.

My 'pro' crew grew extremely worried about a storm brewing off the coast of Portugal, north of Lisbon.

As far as happy-go-innocent Joe was concerned, I was not worried. I was without baggage and without experience. But the so-called 'pros' got the jitters and put on pressure to pull in to Lisbon.

I thought otherwise. Clearly I did not want to take unnecessary risks but I felt we could beat the system and motor sail quickly in the light air to get south of it.

And there is the case that sometimes there can be more risk close to land and going into ports than staying on the open sea. But to keep the others secure and comfortable, I let them think Portugal was an option. It was — but in my heart I was not for stopping unless we had to. Needless to say we beat the weather system.

In my appetite for risk — calculated, I might add — I realise now that my tolerance and comfort levels with it were considerably higher than theirs.

In retrospect it might be fair to say they were 'more normal'. Yet I had felt really comfortable with the voyage that far. In many ways that is a point of difference between individuals. It's not to say one is better than the other; rather that in society it takes (and we need) all kinds.

And it all came good. After getting below the system and picking up the north easterly trade winds which built each day, we left Morocco and Africa to port to arrive after only six-and-a-half days at sea and after covering 1,800 miles.

That was a real achievement.

Life was magic that wonderful morning as we made landfall on Lanzarote and sailed into Puerto Calero in April 2015.

The dream was at the first stage of reality in this magical, balmy venue. For training — and some warm sun — I was joined by family, including my son Cormac, coach Wouter Verbraak and his family.

JOURNEY TO THE EDGE

Wouter is a well-organised, highly capable and calculating Dutchman who lives in the south of England.

He makes a good living from the sport. And good luck to him. Unfairly he shouldered much of the blame in a Volvo Ocean Race disaster when he was navigator on Vestas.

It was shipwrecked in the Indian Ocean and managed to make world headlines and generate a lot of controversy. Had he not crashed the boat on the rocks, he might never have become famous.

The accident was a navigator's error in missing a deep overlay showing the island reefs which were hidden on the top-level electronic chart. Following a major enquiry, there were valuable lessons for all.

Typical of my contrarian spirit, I had also helped Wouter publish a book on his experiences and to tell his side of the story.

We published in both English and Dutch and I wrote the foreword. There is €100 for the reader who finds that book in Dutch in a bookshop in the Netherlands.

Now, with that glitch in his career out of the way, Wouter remains a brilliant navigator. He had completed the two-handed Barcelona around-the-world race on a similar IMOCA boat. When Alex Thomson had to bail out with appendix trouble, he was a last-minute substitute.

Being a rookie, I was fortunate to get a top-level sailor like him and to learn so much from him.

My objective was to move from being an experienced amateur sailor into the ranks of the pros whom I had always admired so much.

Sailing is one of the few global sports where amateurs compete alongside the professionals. However, I was acutely aware of the challenge in getting to professional level and breaking into the pro ranks.

Once, to my horror, this amateur-versus-professional divide was driven home to me as a life-lesson.

And I recall an example in another area altogether where so-called amateurs and professionals meet (or should I say clash?). I had been cast in Bernard Farrell's play 'Canaries' as the Spanish waiter, Carlos, with Dalkey Players.

Knowing I had a media link (as I then worked with the Irish Times) I was asked to get a review of the play by the director.

So in the large open-plan newsroom, I quietly suggested to the Irishman's Diary writer, Kevin Myers, that he review our little play in Dalkey town hall. He became so indignant he climbed on his desk and, much to my embarrassment, roared: "How dare you, how dare you, ask me to do such a thing?" He then proceeded to call me names and berate me in front of all in the newsroom. Only later did I learn that it was a serious insult to ask a professional writer of the theatre to review amateurs' work.

While not quite as dramatic for me, breaking into the world of professional sailing was a similar challenge too.

But this was a real 'pro boat' and to get to that level it was a matter of time on the water.

On arriving at the real Canary Islands at Puerto Calero we were warmly welcomed by Mel Symes who worked with the founding Calero family.

Later, when Nicola arrived, complete with daughter Anna and son Louis, it was not long before we made many friends in that lovely community. Indeed Nicola fell in love with the Calero family home (built and developed by Pepe and Mila) so much that before I knew it, she had made the not-so-little house our own.

Other long-lost friends in Calero included Johnny Morgan, renowned fish merchant and someone I had sailed with on Carlingford Lough many years previously.

We also met Roisin McSorley and her husband Wes. Roisin founded McSorley's Irish Pub in the port which has been bought and sold twice since. Indeed I almost bought it. Now, through their love of sailing and catamarans in particular, they are one of the few really successful day-trip companies I know with their

Catlanza Charter and day-trip sailing operating from Lanzarote and Fuerteventura.

Wes is great company and an even better storyteller. There isn't a tale that any man could tell that Wes wouldn't be able to trump. He certainly could write a screenplay and call his movie 'Adventures In The Caribbean' and I'd predict it would become a blockbuster.

I told him of my time sailing in the US and Caribbean, through islands such as St Martin and St Barts as free ports outside the system. There you'd find a rough group of what I call modern-day pirates.

I'd had a highly lucrative drug smuggling offer some years previously. It was to navigate a yacht from the Caribbean to Canada for $15,000, with $7,000 paid in advance. That was an awful lot of money in the late seventies, particularly for a man in his early twenties.

The prospect of the money and, even more so the adventure of living on the edge, was most attractive. Fortunately I resisted and focused on my sailing and plans for more legal ways to enjoy adventure. That's if you could describe sailing from the US to Ireland in a 16-foot inflatable dinghy as normal — which I did.

If you work in that drug game you need to be tough, mean and nasty to stay ahead — and that's not Enda O'Coineen, although others may have a different view.

The gentleman who made the offer told the extraordinary story of some earlier drug runs. We will call him John for the moment — since he has become a respectable businessman and to identify him, even now, might not be good for his freedom.

In his earlier drug smuggling/courier career as a sailor and navigator he would be given a fast, powerful powerboat. He would drive it with a cargo load of drugs from the Bahamas over to the Florida coast — below the US coastguard radar.

I remember him telling me: "Man, we went straight up the beach at full speed." He described how two men would then race to the beach with chainsaws and a big van would reverse down to the boat.

"They then cut the front half of thc boat off — full with stuff — and loaded it into the van. I got a lump of cash and went my way and they went the other way — all very fast, man."

John got away and was moved up the food-chain towards establishment respectability. He was not so good at the family thing and went through lots of women, some of whom were in the business of sex.

Once before heading solo on a voyage from Halifax, he had a sex shop owner offer to sponsor the shop's name on the bottom of my boat. He also insisted that I be entertained during my last night in port when he sent over three girls, convinced I would never be seen again.

¶ ¶ ¶ ¶

The training and time spent sailing around the Canaries turned out to be invaluable. After going back to work for a while, it was soon time to head north again. Joined by a great British pro-crew Will Ayliffe, it took more than 11 days to get up to Ireland. With light headwinds, it was slow and uneventful.

A few months later I was ready to go back south to the Canaries and across the Atlantic to the Caribbean for a solo race to France in December.

Only the French would organise such an event.

And I was in for some tough sailing.

Many would consider this to be a major risk. But for me, having mastered the sailing and organisation of a 60-foot thoroughbred of the ocean, the risk was not real at all.

And that leads me to the whole issue of managing and understanding risk: the four-letter word which is fundamental to life, civilization and mankind's course through time.

Indeed, I think about risk so much that in the next chapter I take a break from sailing and dive into that whole area.

LESSONS FROM CHAPTER 4

↗ My appetite for risk and my tolerance and comfort levels with it were considerably higher than most people's.

↗ In many ways that is a point of difference between individuals. It's not to say one is better than the other; rather that in society it takes (and we need) all kinds.

Chapter 5
Risk

R ISK is a fascinating concept. For me it is underpins the narrative of my journey all the way to the edge. I also happen to believe it has profound implications and applications for business, personal life and society.

In the understanding and management of risk, I am convinced our society has lost touch with reality.

Back in the 19th century, German physiologist Friedrich Goltz, while carrying out experiments searching for the location of the soul, experimented with frogs. The results and methodology of the experiment were controversial. Essentially, he concluded that if you pop a frog into hot water he will quickly jump to freedom — if he can at all. But drop him into warm water which is gradually heated to boiling point and he will die. I believe, as a civilisation, we are in the warm water.

We need to talk about risk, understand it and keep it in context. The word has been hijacked for other purposes; in its name fundamental freedoms are being lost.

Each day of my solo journey — half of it sailing blind, often at speed in the black of night — was dangerous. You never knew what would happen next. That, to me, is exciting, I have no real desire to do it again but like a risk junkie I became addicted for a time, experiencing the incredible high.

I agree, that's extreme. But it's my calculation, my choice and my decision and I should be free to make it, so long as doing so doesn't put others at risk. The abuse of rules about risk, in the name of safety and security, is strangling society. It is choking the dreams, aspirations and freedoms for which our ancestors fought.

Just consider how, because of so-called risk, children are being stopped from climbing trees. Some are not even allowed to run around the school playground any more for fear they'd fall and cut themselves.

But it is not even that simple. The teacher in charge may be comfortable with the risk; so might the vast majority of parents. But it's that one potential insurance claim that creates fear and paralysis, dictating policy for everyone else.

To me, risk and its understanding is important for a balanced society. The more I research and learn about it, the more I respect it. To understand and measure it has had profound impacts.

Risk comes with reward and has done so right back to hunter-gatherer days. If the man did not go and hunt for food, he and his family starved.

Worth highlighting is the fact that taking risk is not just defined in monetary terms or being able to eat. In my day, if a young man at the dance did not risk rejection and walk across the floor to ask a girl to partner him for the next set, he would never find a woman.

I know, I know — nowadays it's very different — but risk in making connections is still a large factor, regardless of gender. It may just be a finger scroll across Tinder or an online connection that starts it all off. Whatever, it's that spark, that chance encounter, that simple moment that can change the course of each minute and our world. The bottom line is that if you don't ask you don't get.

In my case, even with the experienced pro sailors on board who knew more than me, I was learning that my appetite for — and understanding of — risk was much greater than average. But that is my choice. Not the decision of some rule-maker.

I did not personally consider that I was taking more risk than others. To me it was calculated. But to the others I was in high-risk territory. It's a mindset really.

Everything I have learned about adventure, life and success is about taking risk. Dig deep, peel back the layers and realise it's a subject we should really understand because it's central to our existence, and the mismanagement of it is creating and fortifying nanny states.

¶ ¶ ¶ ¶

The word risk derives from the early Italian "risicare". The literal translation means "to dare". In this sense, risk is a choice rather than a fate. Essentially the actions we dare to take, which depend on how free we are to make choices, are what the story of risk is all about.

And it is that story that helps define what it means to be human; what it means to be alone on the ocean; to adventure, to push the boundaries and challenge the odds.

Adam Smith, widely regarded as the father of modern economics, was keenly aware that our human propensity to take risk propelled economic progress. In that respect he feared society would suffer when the ability to take risk faded. So he was careful to balance moral sentiments against the benefits of a free market.

In other words, when development becomes the by-product of a casino, society is at risk, as the economist John Maynard Keynes said many years later.

Yet our world would be a dull place if people lacked confidence in their own good fortune. Indeed Keynes had to admit: "If human nature felt no temptation to take a chance ....there might not be much investment as a result of cold calculation."

Here's a simple example of what I am talking about.

Hundreds might cross a river every day by boat. Cold calculation might say if you built a bridge these people would use it. But a few hundred toll payers a day would not be economic. However, if you take the risk to build a bridge, the likelihood is that the numbers will move from hundreds to thousands.

I saw the leftovers of the communist system first hand after I went to the Czech Republic not long after the Velvet Revolution. In the Communist system when the Soviets tried to administer uncertainty out of existence through government control and planning, they choked off social and economic progress.

That's another reason why socialism does not work. It kills risk-taking. It's not that I'm against a social society where the successful must look after those who do not make it by paying tax. Rather it's about a balance. If you kill the prospect of reward, you do not understand human nature and therefore you kill, or at least dampen risk.

Again this is not to say that those taking risks should not be managed. What I am saying is that risk has to be carefully managed and understood.

Risk and time are opposite sides of the same coin. If there were no tomorrow there would be no risk.

If I had no prospect of time to complete my solo circumnavigation, I would not have started it in the first place.

Time transforms risk. The nature of the risk is shaped by time. The future is the playing field. Time matters most when decisions are irreversible. And yet many such decisions are made on the basis of incomplete information.

In other words: at some point you have to take a chance.

All the calculations in the world will not be sufficient to manage the risk.

So it is that spark, that extra push, that is the catalyst for the development of civilisations in expanding the boundaries.

I might tack on a wind-shift based on the available weather information which is accurate at the time. However, there may be a pressure change a few hours later and the depression that dictates the wind may divert elsewhere and bring another unpredictable shift. At this stage I have tacked, however.

Irreversibility dominates decisions ranging all the way from altering course to taking the bus or a taxi, to building a factory in Brazil to changing jobs to declaring war. Or deciding to divorce, have an affair, get married or ask that girl, or man, to dance.

As Christianity spread in the western world the will of a single God emerged as the orienting guide to the future. It replaced the miscellany of the deities people had worshipped since the beginning of time. This brought a major shift in perception. The future of life remained a mystery but it was prescribed by a power whose intentions and standards were clear to all who took time to learn them.

Contemplation of the future became a matter of moral behaviour and faith. The future no longer appeared quite as inscrutable, but it was still not susceptible to any mathematical expectation.

I personally see this as having goals and objectives. And I believe in being guided by some powerful force.

Of course, the concept of God is certainly not what we have been led to believe it is — imagining what we cannot imagine.

Since society developed mainly with a focus on one God, instead of lots of them, this is also a factor in the development of civilisation as it is easier to set a focus, create horizons and have objectives.

The sheer power and forces of nature are constantly driven by the positive and the negative, each balancing and fighting the other.

All of this to me is something spiritual.

I believe in a powerful force greater than us individually or as a society. It's something outside of timelines and our boundaries. It's the concept of infinity; the question that has always baffled scientists and philosophers.

Even if God is merely a concept of our imaginations, so be it. We need Him or Her or It. Above all is the spiritual dimension; that which is beyond the beyond and outside what we know or can ever know.

My simple objective to sail solo around the world involved risks. So be it. I would understand, manage and control them.

It's the same with society as a whole. As soon as we started to set goals and objectives, individually and collectively, we advanced from the Stone Age. The concept of replacing randomness with systematic probability generated a radical change in civilisation as we know it.

With that lies the implicit suggestion that the future might be predictable to some degree. That came with the realisation that human beings are not totally helpless in the hands of Fate. Nor is their worldly destiny always determined by God.

The Renaissance and the Protestant Reformation set the scene for the mastery of risk. As mysticism yielded to science and logic, Christopher Columbus was not conducting a Caribbean cruise. He was seeking a new trade route to the Indies.

He took risk with the prospect of getting rich. This was highly motivating; few people get rich without taking a gamble. Columbus was supported and funded by his Spanish king to find wealth and extend influence. With the great risk of voyaging to distance places came great reward. For all Columbus knew at the time, the world might have been flat and he might have fallen off the edge. Research reduced Columbus' risk profile.

Some years ago we recreated one of his journeys from Seville in Spain to my home town of Galway where it was joked Columbus got a road-map of America.

Not quite. As part of his research for his subsequent voyages he travelled up along the western seaboard of Europe with local fishermen. In each new place, in my case Galway, he'd seek out the local monastery where the monks had recorded knowledge. It was here that he came across the story of two mummified

Indians discovered in a dug-out canoe off Galway. That was clear evidence of life on the other side of the Atlantic. The poor unfortunates had gone for a paddle one day and never returned.

So the outsider might have said Columbus and his men were 'stone mad'. But he and his team did not think so. It was research that helped the navigator understand and take the risk that he would find a new world and not fall over the edge.

Yes, Columbus took risk for money but there is more to that blunt statement than meets the eye.

Money comes from trade, which is a mutually beneficial process. It is a transaction in which both parties perceive themselves as wealthier than they were before. If you think about this . . . what a radical idea. Both parties take risk to trade and both are better off. I like to call it 'win-win', and that, to me, is the real upside of risk-taking.

¶ ¶ ¶ ¶

The development of risk management and creating wealth would not have come about only for two activities:

1) Book-keeping;

2) Forecasting.

Put in its simplest form, if you toss a coin 100 times, the theory of probability says that 50 times it will be heads and 50 times tails. This may vary a little, but the more you do it, all other things being equal, it will be half and half. To put it another way: you can safely calculate that around 20 million people have their birthday today and every day — that's based on the world having a population of 7.2 billion.

Placing odds and assessing probability is a fundamental of risk.

I was doing it at a basic level on my boat, during various adventures and at different levels in my life. We all do. That's what makes us individuals with freedoms to choose and live life as it needs to, and should, be lived.

Insurance and the industry around it, is totally built on understanding risk and probability. Before insurance came along a ship might sail with a cargo, the loss of which in a storm would mean devastation for the owner, his family, village and community. It would take generations, if ever, to recover. But with the probability that if 100 ships sail and 5 are lost — a 5 percent chance — the insurance premium might be 7pc of the value. So the underwriter would be ahead on the law of averages and the ship owner could build and sail again.

Entire civilisations have been lost and societies have gone backwards because risk was not understood or managed.

Indeed the reason the kingdom of Siam survived for thousands of years was that the monarch had several wives and families in totally different locations. So if one family got wiped out, by disease or an enemy, there would be another, elsewhere, to continue the dynasty.

In the next chapter I look at where risk management and understanding it was critical to my solo navigation.

It was my freedom, my choice and my risk. And I understood it.

Now let me, complete with my own understanding of risk and its history, highlight some examples in a simplistic view of how society handles risk:

*The use of contraceptives paved the way for family planning and reduced the risk of unwanted pregnancies.

*Companies and individuals are scored and rated for risk. It's a massively complex industry, now driven by data, analysis and deep drill-downs into every aspect of the enterprise.

*Since it is said that nine-out-of-10 new enterprises fail, a good way to reduce the associated risk is to take a proven business formula that works and roll it out. The franchising business model is a good example. I like it because it allows the individual to partner, retain independence, drive their own destiny and yet massively reduce the risk to their business. Mind you, in doing that they give away a share of their upside.

*To give the job to someone you know might be considered wrong and unfair. It happens with business people who want to reduce the risk of hiring somebody or using something they don't know anything about, which could place them at greater risk.

It's a matter of balance and it's the freedom of the business owner or manager to make his own decisions based on the risk and the fundamental rule of society that everyone gets an equal opportunity.

The hiring process reminds me of a friend who was interviewing candidates. He got a call from another friend lobbying him for the job.

"And why should he get the job?" he asks.

"Oh! He's from Cork," came the response.

These are simple examples and trains of lateral thinking from my personal Journey to the Edge. If we look right through life, in the end, it all comes back to risk.

Another marker in the development of freedom was that success was based on merit, promotion and rewarding the risk takers. To put it another way: in selecting the best soccer team to represent your country or the best representative for the Olympics, would you pick the sons or daughters of previous medal winners? Certainly not. Unless they prove themselves to be better than anyone else.

In the United States, more than 50pc of all wealth is inherited. That means ultimately it's not the best or most deserving who get the jobs. It is, rather, those who inherit or have the connections. Sure, we all try to do the best we can for our offspring but if levels of inherited wealth continue at this rate we will find ourselves in a lose-lose situation.

In a sense what happened with the French Revolution could impact in another way in the US as fewer and fewer people hold more and more of the wealth.

To give you a more practical example of risk-gone-mad: recently in Lanzarote, Nicola and I were renting a bike from a German operator. We opted not to take helmets since we were just cycling around the neighbourhood.

The operator lectured us on the importance of helmets. He would not rent the bikes to us without them. Fine. We took the helmets but, when out of sight, removed them. It was the freedom, the breeze, hair flying, memories of carefree childhood days and all that.

I have crashed bikes many times, never wearing a helmet. I have even done somersaults over the handlebars but somehow I survived. Yes, I did cut and hurt myself. Yet, in all of these situations, given the relatively slow speed of a bike and my reactions, a helmet would have been a waste of time.

Out of sight of the Lanzarote renter, I felt better for discarding the helmet. It was almost a personal statement of freedom. This was my decision, my risk and my responsibility, my independence. Sure, if on a risky open road I might have considered wearing that helmet. But it would be my decision, not one by a rental operator or lawmaker.

It is important to point out I am not saying you shouldn't wear a helmet. Rather it is/was my personal decision. In all probability, if I were riding outside my comfort zone, going fast or where there was great risk, I would wear one. But I have to stress it would be my call and I would not attempt to influence anyone else in doing so.

¶ ¶ ¶ ¶

Sailing my IMOCA 60 alone off the coast of Brittany on the way to the start, I was running around the deck and rig with no lifejacket on.

I was mobile, happy, agile and in my view quite safe. Indeed a lifejacket would have made movement more difficult and perhaps even less safe. As I was being filmed from a helicopter, I got lots of comments and criticism about why I was not wearing a lifejacket.

Again it was my decision. My freedom. My call.

In extreme conditions I would wear safety gear but it was a decision I had to make, not somebody looking at helicopter videos.

Sometimes in life we are successful because we have to be: the risk of failure is too great to contemplate.

When I set up business in Prague for the first time I slept in the office.

Each evening the staff would leave me behind and each morning I was there when they came in — having camped on the desk. This achieved two things. It saved money and it sent a message to all that this business had to work. The risk of failure was simply not considered.

Few people with a young family, a mortgage and other responsibilities would have taken such a risk but I did. That was my choice. The risk was calculated. The reward was success.

To get started I needed credit from a bank. It was not forthcoming. The fact I had had a good repayment history back home did not matter. They eventually came up with money when I did not need it. But I decided to draw it down anyway — at high interest — and repaid it some time later.

I learned that the Czech banks had no credit risk system for sharing clients' histories between themselves. This was clearly a market need and a fundamental part of a functioning economy. For that reason I decided to set up a credit bureau. Today it is a multi-million euro business.

In the US you can have instant credit but if you default it goes on the system and it can take years to clear your name. Europe was behind, while nothing like that existed in the Czech economy at all.

It's bizarre that if we deposit cash in a bank it is confidential to you and the lending institution. However, if we borrow we give up certain rights. The banks share information on your credit to protect them and the market.

Initially my plan was to model the new Czech credit reference business on the successful Irish Bureau. I wanted them to partner. I also looked around the world to copy and improve on the best models. But the Irish Credit Bureau at the time, while successful and cash-rich, was too involved in internal politics between shareholders and management and could not look outside Ireland.

In the end I found Larry Howell on his mobile in the back of a boat. Larry was then president of Trans Union International out of Chicago. After that I linked up with Carlo Gheradi, CEO of CRIF in Bologna, Italy.

Both men supported the idea. It was a new market for them. They took the risk and eventually bought me out so that was a 'win-win'. Kilcullen Kapital made some money and they now have the Czech and Slovak Credit Bureaux as part of a successful global business.

Getting the bureau going was a big challenge and one of my proudest business achievements. It involved bringing together the risk managers, IT directors, and commercial managers of all the large banks to share information.

Every two weeks we would meet in the grandiose chambers, complete with chandeliers, of the Czech Banking Association. And while we had got them all to agree to get the business going, it involved a committee of more than 20. It plodded along.

The delays did not deter me from a planned five-month break to live on a boat in the Caribbean with my then wife Suzanna and three daughters.

But on return, the agenda had moved little. So, at the next meeting, I showed all the bankers my holiday photos. Then I aborted the meeting, much to their shock and horror. If I had been a fellow Czech they would probably have thrown me out. However, they did not quite know what to do with a foreigner. So I called an emergency informal breakfast meeting of the CEOs of the largest banks in the country. I was supported by Irish American Jack Stack who then ran Cesky Sportilena, the largest Czech bank employing more than 10,000.

And though the CEOs were so far removed from the process of setting up the credit sharing bureau, the fact they were meeting at all and taking an interest made the rest realise we needed to move forward. We did eventually launch the business and service. It was a fascinating process and again it allowed bankers to be scientific about risk.

In itself it was an extraordinary study. What I'm about to say might be a little politically incorrect but so be it.

In the UK, for example, we learned that Protestants in communities were more likely to default than Catholics.

It seems Catholics tended to be more connected with communities, had larger families and did not move around as much. So defaulting was going more against their peer group. Protestants, though you would expect them to be more prudent, tended to have smaller families, were more likely to move and were less connected with their communities.

We also found that people with red cars were more inclined to default than those with green vehicles simply because they were likely to be more extrovert and adventurous.

The Czech Republic and her people were successful under Communism almost to spite the communists. And while one has to admire the ideals of pure Communism, as a system to govern society it failed. It does not take into account the key elements of human nature: diversity, motivation and risk.

Let me, finally, outline what in my view is the stupidity of society about risk. Take the example of the Atlantic Youth Trust, a charity I'm involved with.

Essentially our mission is to connect youth with the ocean and adventure. It is also to assist with youth development and reconciliation. In Ireland the state pays about €250,000 a year to lock up boys between the ages of 13 and 18. Granted, about 20 percent cannot be 'saved'. But the other 80 percent end up in detention because society is afraid — rightly in some ways — of the risk they'd pose if free. Their families cannot handle them. The gardai cannot handle them.

So we send them away for detention at a time when they are not even old enough to be criminals. Of course, when most of them come out, aged 18 or so, they have effectively learned to be criminals — in many cases for the rest of their lives. Which means they become a constant burden on society.

So we are saying to the state: "Give us €2.5m a year for 10 boys, for example." We have the captive environment of a boat, the maritime backdrop and the attraction that the boat can travel to exotic locations. We could employ top-class professionals to manage the youths and pay a dividend to the State by doing it better.

The logic is overpowering. The statistics of such activity in other countries show the repeat-offence rate is significantly less. Society is saved the cost of people being constantly jailed for the rest of their lives.

But institutions and mid-management won't take risk. We will succeed in this, eventually, I hope, but it's an uphill struggle. Mid-management are more focused on keeping their own 'turf' and budgets than actually taking the risk to do it differently and better. The institutions of state become settled in their ways because of the risk-averse culture.

Be it solo around the world, starting a family, a business or simply going the pub for a pint, it all involves risk.

And so, after all that it's back to the voyage.

After completing my training voyages up and down to the Canaries and around Ireland, I prepared to set sail.

LESSONS FROM CHAPTER 5
↗ The understanding, quantifying and management

of risk is a fundamental building block of society and civilisation as we have come to know them.

↗ After all the research and preparation, at some point you have to push the boat out and take a risk.

When I eventually set off, I now realise I had never been so happy to be on my own. The professional crew I'd hired was a disaster.

Chapter 6
Qualifying Against The Odds

SETTING out solo for the first time across the Atlantic to arrive in the Bay of Biscay and the French coastline in December was a fearsome prospect.

That said, preparing to start was an even more frightening challenge. You simply could not make up what happened.

In addition to full-on sailing and intense boat preparation I had to deal with drunkards, a bully and a sponsor who had no money and was delusional.

After 11 days at sea crossing the Atlantic from the Canaries — fast by any standards — we made our landfall on the island of St Martin.

This was a two-handed and final preparation on this amazing ocean racing machine to go solo. When I eventually set, I now realise I had never been so happy to be on my own. The professional crew I'd hired was a disaster.

We were advised St Martin was more practical and economical for preparations than neighbouring St Barts, where the Transatlantic Race was to start.

St Barts is an incredibly beautiful, expensive and exclusive sort of French island. Such is its reputation for luxury that employees of the respective teams' corporate sponsors were shy to be seen there, in case the public thought they were living too good a life on company money. And they were.

Sadly the following year all the islands were devastated by a hurricane.

We landed at the Dutch side, St Martin, in early December 2015. With a deep keel our berthing options were limited inside the lagoon. I was shocked when told the marina berth visitor price was almost $1,000 a night.

A venue generally frequented by billionaires, it included the super yacht built for the late Steve Jobs of Apple. Since our boat had a depth of almost five metres, there were limited options on where we could berth safely.

The marina manager quipped: "You seem like an ordinary old millionaire." Officially he could not give me a discount but I enjoyed a substantial reduction due to his 'low-season' rate in high season.

On the first night after landing, my crewman for the Atlantic got seriously drunk. All his aggression and personal issues came out. I had endured him during the 11-day crossing but managed to grin and bear it. I was dependent on him so it had been a delicate few days while we began preparations to start the solo back to France.

This was not pleasure sailing. This was goal-orientated focus to succeed. So I tolerated him as a sort of punishment and necessity to achieve a goal. I was also in the learning phase of running an ocean racing boat.

Through personal recommendations I had taken him on board as a crewman for training for the two-handed delivery leg. He turned out to be temperamental, and the voyage was not only a test of sailing and boat but a personal horror story.

Being a little behind schedule, we had under a week to prepare for the race back to France and thereby to complete qualification for the Vendée. Clearly, I survived — but it was a nightmare. Ultimately I had to trick him into helping me sail solo from St Barts when it came time to start the race.

I was exhausted, finally, leaving St Barts; 15 boats had entered the race and I was the final of seven to make it to the start line, albeit a day late. Many had dropped out en route over various problems and storms.

I was really delighted to get away. Not only had I succeeded in qualifying and starting a major solo Transatlantic race, it was a critical juncture for the Vendée Globe too.

And it was an escape from the crew.

To complicate matters, the sponsor was not a sponsor at all. That was despite me putting all his graphics on the boat at great expense after the first dispatch were lost by the courier company. He had promised $50,000 but was something of a Walter Mitty character. He also got quite drunk with my crew and, in the end, never came up with the money.

The entire period was comical. There was high tension: there was desperate struggle with the crewman and I had to cope with a deluded sponsor as well.

Much later, I was fooled again and made a large investment of my own and my partner's cash in his business. All would be lost.

¶ ¶ ¶ ¶

Anyway, here is the first of my logs at sea. Right through the race and the main Vendée event, it was a condition of participation that regular reports were made.

More by accident than design, the daily logs — now blogs — gained great traction on social media. Even if no one read them they were a great regular therapy for me and a formal record for now.

△ Log 1 — Day 2

It's a beautiful evening here as we sail upwind with full main and J2. My Chapter of the Atlantic Residents Association — ARA are happy out and have determined that:

'I am a Wave of the Sea
And the Foam of the Wave
And the Wind of the Foam
And the Wings of the Water'
(Joseph Plunkett)

We seem to be catching the fleet a little, having started more than a day late. Our modest objective is just to finish and mobilise the Pensioners of Port La Forêt to cast off their sticks and dance for joy in the streets if we make it.

So far, it's straight-line sailing and, while getting a little cooler, it's still really hot by comparison with what's ahead.

Whether a compliment or an insult, I'm not sure, but Jarleth Vahey of Mayo extraction had the local West Indian watchers of our work in stitches laughing when he said you would need a "wheelbarrow to support the cohunes of the skipper".

That was to do with the boat being under a crane while we worked into the night. Carl, our genius mechanic, was stretched underneath fixing the sail drive. The same Mr Vahey (a Portsmouth resident of Mayo extraction where somehow an 'F' became a 'V') had dropped everything and flown overnight to bring parts from the UK.

After many phone calls, I'd found the parts supplier drinking pints in Croydon on Friday night.

The punters and the 'hurlers on the ditch' said it would be impossible to make the start. However, we moved mountains as problem after problem came at us. We were 'hungry for solutions'.

The final delay was a concern about the keel. A wide-angled diver photo under water showed the back tip of it as if a big chunk had come away. It sent my unstable bully (on whom I remained dependent) into orbit as a drama queen when in fact, if you looked at a picture of the entire keel, it was minuscule. The underwater wide angle close-up shot had totally distorted it. I talked with structural specialists — including Merf Owen the designer — and it became evident it was not a reason to abort sailing.

Men had become mice.

My shore team were in such a negative downward spiral that the only way I could motivate them to carry out the final preparations was deceit.

I had to let them think I was going to sail the boat to Guadeloupe, 150 miles upwind. There they wanted to check the boat and do an NDT (Non-Destructive Test) on the bulb and keel before, and if, starting the race.

Besides being completely unnecessary, such was their knowledge of NDT testing, that it would have been pointless. You cannot do an NDT on lead.

This prompts the awful question: What is the ultimate definition of Irish innocence? Trainee nuns in a factory in Mayo making condoms under the belief that they were making sleeping bags for mice?

Anyway... the team worked hard but, in my view, the last few days represented complete burnout and loss of confidence in the boat and skipper — who ultimately must take the decisions and responsibility.

And now, looking astern as the sun sinks in over the horizon as it does every day, I never cease to be amazed that I am here at all.

'The silver apples of the moon
The golden apples of the sun'
(WB Yeats)

I'm amazed at our universe, the vastness of the ocean, the simple beauty of the sea and the madness of our human being on this little planet. Indeed, I feel it's a great freedom, privilege and honour to be here alone — away from it all.

Now we sail into the night, seeking the moon do a bit of howling and perhaps practise my new trumpet.

And finally, a big thanks to all who have supported the project, allowing me to sail my dream which I hope will boost the Atlantic Youth Trust charity and grow Currency House Bank.

I wrote the preceding log in total innocence. The tragedy, I was to learn later, was that Currency House was not a proper bank and my so-called sponsor had misled me. Innocently, I was headed out into the Atlantic expecting that his money would arrive back home to help fund our campaign costs.

¶ ¶ ¶ ¶

I had formed the Atlantic Residents Association in my mind to manage matters when alone. It had its own president, ministers and officers who would deliberate with great intensity on matters. It was sort of myself talking with myself and other self, if you follow my drift.

¶ ¶ ¶ ¶

Δ Log 2 — Day 3

Just another old day in Paradise.

Champagne sailing, we are close to reaching 11 knots and happy out steering north east — roughly pointed at the Azores. From the weather routing (thanks to Alex Thomson for guidance during pre-start) I favour the more southern route. It's a little safer, more conservative and hopefully warmer. If hungrier for speed, I would have more sail up and perhaps go more northwards. But sure, we're just grand.

There is a beautiful evening sun on the quarter. Away from so-called civilisation, during this brief interlude, I have not a care in the world. Myself and my other-selves are in our element. Unlike other singlehanded sailors I do not suffer from insanity — I enjoy every minute of it.

This is ocean sailing at its best. Totally self-contained. To be a pilot on one of these 60 foot creatures of the ocean is a rare privilege. I savour it all as one of the world's last great freedoms.

The Atlantic Residents Association met this morning (the meeting took place in my head — just so you know).

Being late on the line, playing catch-up with the other skippers is not easy. However, I have emailed all with a New Race Rule and briefed them on the decision of the meeting: they all must buy the last skipper home a drink and share their girlfriends for a night. (Just kidding on the last one, I've got my girl). And toast:

'And to the ship that goes
And the wind that blows
And the lass who loves a sailor'
(Charles Dibdin)

All skippers have been accepted as members of the Atlantic Residents Association. This is an exclusive club which has seven members. Mind you, I am reluctant to join a club that would have me as a member (in the tradition of Groucho Marx). At the meeting this morning, seven serious questions were asked:

1. What are the 7 Wonders of the world?
2. Why did Snow White have 7 dwarfs?
3. Why does the World have 7 seas?
4. Why are there 7 deadly sins?
5. Why does the 7th son of a 7th son have special powers?
6. What is the 7th heaven?
7. Why are 7 IMOCA 60ies left racing from 15 entries?

The following is the official membership list of the association — the remaining competitors in the Race:

1. Sebastian Jose
2. Paul Meilhart SMA
3. Morgan Lagravière
4. Thomas Ruyant, Le Souffle du Nord
5. Fabrice Amédéo
6. Eric Holden
7. Enda O'Coineen, Currency House Kilcullen

All should be congratulated on membership of this unique club. So now we are Seven.

Another rule is that anyone who takes membership of this distinguished group too seriously will automatically be expelled.

Furthermore, the first item on the agenda for our next meeting is 'The Split'.

Hopefully, all new members will remain on board despite The Split and we will all meet in Port La Forêt with the brass band — and when the Fat Lady starts singing.

¶ ¶ ¶ ¶

And so, I settled into sailing. I was fired up to catch the other boats. Most important from a personal viewpoint was not to be last, even though I started a day late. But, as we moved gradually north into the winter and colder weather, little did I know what lay ahead.

Δ Day 6

Again brilliant sailing as we reach further east. The weather routing is telling us to keep south — hopefully to get around those nasty systems up there. It's still warm but each day you can feel the temperature drop some. And so as I practise the trumpet I am making music (of sorts) while the sun shines.

Sole sailors 'blow their own trumpets' and I have been blowing mine with a lot of time for thinking. If "two's company, three is a crowd, what's one?" All alone here on the ocean, I am answering questions that have not been asked. Would that make me a philosopher of the ocean? Or is it just insanity when I hear those voices, talk with them and then when they answer back?

And back on my trumpet, rarely can you find a better

place to learn a new instrument. Even the flying fish are shocked with the noise, although they still hit the passing yacht like bullets and continue landing on deck like Jihadists.

'Oh, When the Saints
Oh, When the Saints
Go Marching In....'

And, just in case you're wondering, to complete my band on board I also have a mini harmonica and a bodhrán (an Irish drum) to beat on. It is made from goat skin. Now, sailing along with my complete Atlantic Residents Association Band, I feel I am diagonally parked in a parallel universe. Even the neighbours have been complaining about the noise.

Meanwhile, back racing... as the wind moves up and down we've had the water ballast in and out and several sail changes making for a busy day. Going into darkness now we are settled in with a full main and J1, a large genoa. Though tempting, I tend to avoid sail changes at night. I also find I am doing stuff I would never have thought possible on my own up to now. As I have been sailing with an experienced crew I would generally have left it to them.

But now I have to do it and love it. That is the wonderful challenge and achievement of going solo. That said, it's not human nature to be so alone for so long. Which makes me wonder about it all.

Of course, we can think of it as the essence of life and sure, if you set out on a journey and don't know where you're going you'll never get there.

Now, sailing into darkness, your humble skipper's only ambition is to get to Port La Forêt (wherever that is) on this wonderful 60 footer (one for every year of my life, almost).

Let's see what the dawn brings.

Δ Day 7

Cut my finger this morning. I should be upset, but not really. I was mighty pleased to use my elaborate and massive first aid-kit for the first time.

While only a simple bandage was needed, to actually use what is basically a mini mobile hospital, costing a small fortune, gave cause for satisfaction. From morphine to stuff to sew myself up with and everything exotic in between, it's good to know it's there. There is even a great little book on how to be a good doctor to myself.

However, it leaves out the 'head' bit. Most GPs these days seem more like psychiatrists and head fixers rather than catering for bodily ailments when people come with their problems. Medicine has become so advanced it's impossible for a doctor to examine someone without finding something wrong with them. We have come to expect having something wrong as the norm and someone to complain about — instead of taking it ourselves.

Anyway, my 'cut' pumped red healthy blood. I got it from the sharp blade of the hydro generator when a wave rolled as I was lifting it up over the stern. The converter box had become extremely hot, so I thought it best to give the charger a rest. I am also sobered by the thought that the converter blew up on one of the other boats. There are two. They generate more than 40 amps and make you totally self-sufficient in energy. This is mighty and means you can go on forever and again.

Now getting into mid-voyage, it seems like I am living in eternity as the hours and days roll on.

We are under full main and J1 Genoa, surfing along between 13 and 15 knots at 100 degrees true wind. It would seem prudent to stay a little south.

You can feel the air change and new weather coming; there is a big storm brewing. On a regular basis, I get up and walk around the deck to find things out of place, something exposed; I try constantly to be alert to potential damage and breakages.

'Molly Malone', my aptly named self-steering system, is the lady on this ship on whom I am most dependent. If it goes when the wind is above 15 knots the weather helm is so strong on the boat that it is almost impossible to steer. And do you know the best navigation advice I ever got? Ever?

It was:

"Steer around the rocks."

'And she wheeled her wheelbarrow,

through streets broad and narrow,

crying cockles and mussels

Alive, Alive oh...'

Despite email and fancy sat phones it's still lonely out here. I am on my own. My little space on the boat is small, but this Atlantic Ocean of ours is so vast and has so many personalities. I have no idea what is happening outside the boat compound. As the world rolls on it's becoming sort of claustrophobic.

For my current reading material, I am delving into 'A Modest Proposal' written by Jonathan Swift in the year 1732: 'An Examination of Certain Abuses, Corruptions and Enormities in the City of Dublin.'

Now, going into darkness I have just been on deck, reefed the main, taken down the J1 Genoa and put up the A7 downwind sail (all a lot of work for one dude) as the wind draws aft and the pressure builds.

Δ Day 8

Today, alone on this vast ocean, I was almost insane. Albert Einstein defined insanity it as the person who keeps doing the same thing while expecting something different.

On the foredeck, I kept recoiling (by hand) the old-style headsail furler — as distinct from the more efficient Karver ones — and kept repeating it. Yet I failed to solve the problem.

It would be solved temporarily and then it would revert. And I kept applying the same solution. This Genoa is the main working headsail. It's one that needs to be replaced. Without it, I have slowed down. The flogging and danger of further snarl-up inhibits other sails I can set. As well as having broken two batters in the main, it is restricting me to sailing with at least two reefs. It does not help.

Eventually a link to sanity returned with something different happening. The problem may be solved well enough to get me to the finish. I have also been in touch with the race-committee exploring options to do a pit-stop at the Azores for repairs. And, sure, it's a nice place on the way. They might even have an Irish pub? This is allowed while staying in the race, according to the rules. Also, since this is a non-stop race, like a non-stop airline flight, I would like to know how you stop?

Here in the black of night, perhaps like the astronauts when they landed in their capsules in the ocean from space, I sit here in a tiny cocoon. The hatch is sealed to protect from the following sea. Like the space capsule it has a porthole. I sit on the seat, which doubles up as a bed, staring at a range of panels on night time infrared.

Up top the small J3 jib and two reefs in the main are set. Here below, my key indicators are true wind speed: currently 27 knots. Boat speed: 17 knots and surging, compass 30 degrees; true wind angle 131 degrees and so on. The only sounds are the gushing of the ocean as we surf down waves. There is the occasional bang into a wave and constant movement in every direction.

Sitting here I always wear oilskin trousers and boots

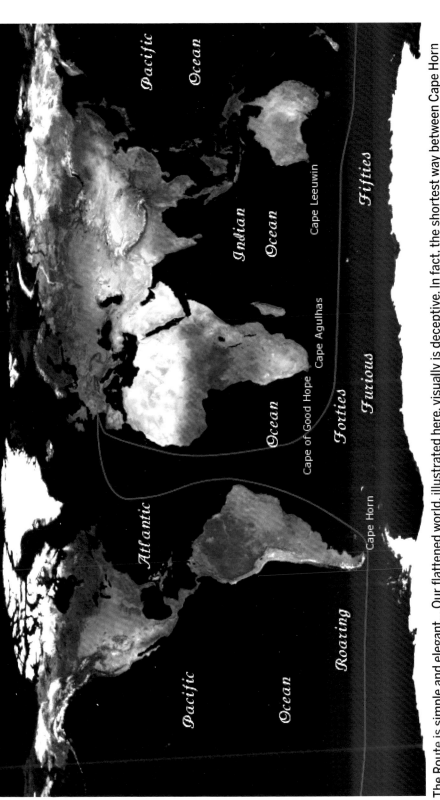

The Route is simple and elegant... Our flattened world, illustrated here, visually is deceptive. In fact, the shortest way between Cape Horn (Chile) and Cape Leeuwin (Australia) is through the melting South Pole. For good measure, adding the third great Cape, the Cape of Good Hope, at each of the landmarks, I poured a wee drop of whiskey provided by Kieran Jameson, Aidan McManus and Howth YC friends. When you realise that two-thirds of the world is covered by ocean — as you try to navigate it — the vast scale of the undertaking, solo, comes into perspective. In truth, it's smarter to fly and there is no logic to the logic...

With Neil Jordan and Damien Meaney "officially" opening The Irish Village and the Irish Embassy Pub in Haiti. Trying to help this challenged country was an extraordinary adventure. With Conchur de Barra, a great partner, it started in seeking to make a real contribution after the earthquake and ended when a security guard was shot dead.

Look what my parents Maureen and Charlie started (and they each had big families — do the maths!) Every two years we get together with three boys and five girls (sadly we lost the youngest Frances and her husband, Tom) and some 28 grandchildren and — with the great grands — still counting...
Sitting (left to right): Moushumi Moran, Nicola McGuire, Priya Moran, Johan Huurman, Mairead Huurman, Cormac & Enda O'Coineen, Tim & Aurelia Huurman, Mona McDonnell, Eoin Murt Rabbitt, Pauline Moran, Elaine & Carla Huurman.
Next row: Carlos & Nicolas Ruiz, Mark & Shay Moran, Cormac Rabbitt, Sean McGuire,

With my daughter Aisling a few hours before the opening of The Irish Embassy in Haiti. One time the Haitian police were afraid to enter to arrest a member of the kitchen staff for a crime because they thought it was a real Embassy! And other times it was used for a church service on Sunday mornings...

Annmarie Bowring, Aifric Rabbitt, Maire McGucken, Saffron Brady, Laurann Rabbitt, Charlie Bowring, Charlie Huurman, Carol, Kevin & Rossa Moran, Saoirse O'Coineen, Roisin & Arthur Courtney, Niamh Haghandish, Mary Rabbitt and Frances Brady.
Back row: Sarah Beirne, Edel & Senan Moran, Daisy Huurman, Alice Bowring, Johnny & Conor Beirne, Aisling O'Coineen, Sarah Bowring, Sean Bowring, Charlie Bowring, James McDonnell, Sean MacDonnchadha, Alison McDonnell, Claire McDonnell & Eduardo Arandilla, Susanna O'Coineen, Peter Bowring, Roger Courtney, Ken Moran, Ramtin Haghandish, Martin McDonnell and Thom Brady.

John Killeen, Enda Kenny (Taoiseach), Knut Frostad (Race CEO) and I with the Volvo Ocean Race Trophy. In 2012 we brought it to Galway for the second time, generating a strong enonomic benefit to the region. It was organised in the teeth of a recession and run on a voluntary basis — though it took us another two years to resolve all outstanding bills. It was a proud achievement (sorting the bills!)

My daughters Aisling, Roisin and Saoirse and wife Nicola Mitchell who took me back after being alone at sea for so long...

In Belfast, with the Titanic Quarter backdrop, campaigning for an Atlantic Youth development Tall Ship. Our message was that Belfast was obsessed with restoring history but needed to build the future and connect youth with adventure and the ocean.

I took the St Patrick's Brass Band, founded by my grandfather around 1898, to play on the Aran Islands for the first time at the WIORA Championships.

Our training leg around Ireland included Aran and special efforts to connect with youth. Also, a lady whose name I never got and remains a mystery, presented me with a bottle of Holy Water. It worked and I was happy to take every spiritual insurance possible. The bottle completed the voyage alongside my whiskey. And photographed with me at Kilronan Pier, from left: Áine Nic Giolla De, Clíona Ní Dhuileain, Éabha Ní Dhuileain, Sieanna Ní Fhlaithearta, Caelain Cullen Quinn, Eoghan Ó Conghaile, Senan Ó Giolla De agus Cian Ó Duilleain.

In Kiev, capital of the Ukraine with the Taras Shevchenko statue. In 1847 he was convicted for writing in the Ukrainian language, promoting the independence of Ukraine and ridiculing the members of the Russian Imperial House. Little has changed and this was a tough country to do business in.

Cathal Friel, on board from Belfast to Dublin with Rockabill Lighthouse astern. A good friend and his company, Raglan Capital supported the adventure.

All the Vendée Skippers were invited to the Élysée Palace in Paris to meet French President François Hollande. That's Prince Albert of Monaco in the background. We chatted about whiskey while waiting for the President, who was delayed by a terrorist bomb. I promised a bottle of whiskey, which I would bring as cargo around the world, to Albert for his collection (*see final pictures*). Meanwhile, President Hollande equated the Vendée with challenge and explained the French people's love for the event which pitted man against the elements, romance, adventure and all that...

Steve Fisher, Chairman of the New Zealand Spirit of Adventure Trust, who adopted me in New Zealand. It's a charity with which our Atlantic Youth Trust has a lot in common and a group we regard as a 'role model'.

With Sean Melly and Bobby Kerr after a Newstalk chat show where we talked about the Senate and the need for politicians to go to school to learn how to manage civil servants when they become ministers...

A cartoon illustration from our programme where school kids followed the voyage around the world as an education tool in geography, science and adventure.

Marcus Hutchinson who played a key role in professionally managing the campaign, a friend and a valuable connection into the world of French sailing.

Angelique and Francois Buoy (Chairman of Le Souffle du Nord) who came to New Zealand in support. Their son Max worked on the rebuilding project and son Roman, came to the Aran islands to teach sailing.

With broadcaster Ryan Tubridy who came for a sail on Dublin Bay during our circumnavigation of Ireland...

Sylvian Derreumaux, CEO of Le Souffle du Nord (Wind of the North) based in Lille, France. I was honoured to partner and be their Ambassador to finish the Circumnavigation.

"I have spread my dreams under your feet. Tread softly because you tread on my dreams."
W.B. Yeats

Enda O'Coineen

VENDÉE
LE DÉPARTEMENT

The immortal words of W.B. Yeats, a reminder to myself and visitors on the deck of the boat, that I had the honour to navigate the oceans of the world but to tread carefully...

Prior to starting the 2016 Vendée Globe, skippers, competitors and comrades gather. Each one of us had a unique journey to the start. While solo, there was deep personal emotional connectivity. For most it was an incredible challenge just to get to the line in motivating and winning support for the massive challenge ahead.

Photographed at the Paris Stock Exchange with two men in suits: (left) Lionel Parriset, of Les Sables-d'Olonne and (right) Yves Auvinet, President SAEM Vendée. And the 29 Solo Skippers: Conrad Colman (NZ), Rich Wilson (USA), Thomas Ruyant

(FR), Alan Roura (SU), Vincent Riou (FR), Kito de Pavant (FR), Paul Meilhat (FR), Stéphane Le Diraison (FR), Enda O'Coineen (IRL) Fabrice Amedeo (FR), Éric Bellion (FR), Romain Attanasio (FR), Jérémie Beyou (FR), Bertrand de Broc (FR), Louis Burton (FR), Didac Costa (FR), Sébastien Destremau (FR), Jean-Pierre Dick (FR), Yann Eliès (FR), Nándor Fa (HU), Pieter Heerema (NED), Sébastien Josse (FR), Morgan Lagravière (FR), Tanguy de Lamotte (FR), Jean Le Cam (FR), Armel Le Cléac'h (FR), Kojiro Shiraishi (JAP), Arnaud Boissières (FR) and Alex Thompson (UK).

Kilcullen Match Racing off Cork Harbour, (representing The Royal Galway YC), with Hugo Boss, Alex Thomson and Steward Hosford, (representing Royal Cork YC) for the Historic Galway Plate, first raced for in 1834.

《《《 Testing the Survival Suit, one of many preparations necessary, which included intense self-help medical training, the ability to stich oneself and perform operations...

On the wind...

Taking a swim off Gozo, after sailing in less than seven days in the first training leg from Southampton to the Canaries.

Looking astern, in the deep Atlantic, with the feet up!

A stray racing pigeon, lost and found at sea.

ready to go; I pop up every now and then with a flashlight to check things out.

You are living on the edge.

There is no visibility ahead and you have no idea what is going to happen next.

Your mind and body become at one with the boat — so even when napping, a change of movement or sound will alert you (I hope).

Sometimes in these conditions I am afraid to sleep... which reminds me, did anyone put the cat out?

¶ ¶ ¶ ¶

While my logs just reflected part of the picture and my internal journey as it were, the weather was creating havoc with the other competitors. Three boats had to abandon for various reasons, including broken rudders and gear failure. The most dramatic of them was Paul Meilhart on SMA.

An accomplished sailor, he would have been among the favourites to do well. And unbeknownst to me, it involved the same storm I experienced further south. He was on deck when a wave picked him up and smashed him down, breaking his pelvis in the process.

In my case, rather than go on deck in the storm, I stayed below thinking it would be better to let the head flog to pieces rather than trying to take it down. In many ways this was more psychologically demanding. In retrospect it was a sign of maturity and might have saved my life.

In a dramatic rescue, Paul was eventually taken to the Azores while his boat was left to drift for several days at the mercy of the elements. She eventually worked her way north. It was the SMA project manager, Marcus Hutchinson, who led the rescues and saved the boat. Eventually they got her back to France with a lot of damage. Happily, with an extensive repair, Paul recovered and went back to sea again with success — until his next drama in the Vendée — but that's another story.

△ Day 9

Being honest, I was scared. Through the early morning, it blew up to 40 knots — I ran off before it. The waves trundled after us, sometimes as high as double-decker buses and predictable like the 7A. However, it's the odd rogue wave, against the flow that catches you unaware.

Eventually last night's storm abated. I dozed off to sleep and awoke about 90 minutes later. The miserable grey dawn had arrived like a black and white movie. Now the days are so short they morph into the night. It can be hard to tell the difference. The wind had dropped back to 15 knots. Like getting a thrill from being the last on a plane, or doing something that's against the rule, it is the living on the edge which brings the kicks. Somehow I am not sure if that's healthy, even if I have survived, insofar as my hair gets greyer.

This morning I had three tasks on sunrise. The question was: in which order? One was my ritual bowl of porridge, the other a sail change and the third to have a dump — though the least said about that the better.

However, I should mention one seldom-mentioned fact that has revolutionised ocean racing. It is the arrival of the biodegradable plastic bag and wipes — not around when I was a lad.

Anyway, I went for the sail change first. This involved dragging the large headsail on deck and other preparations. Then when ready to go I had my porridge. It was just as well, since within an hour the wind was back up to 25 knots plus, so I abandoned the sail change.

Now my mood moved to survival. Not much succour from romance and poetry. Overhead the rain pounds like pellets, I have never seen as much in one deluge from the heavens. From tropics, through autumn and now winter, we have had three seasons in 10 days. So spring must be just around the corner? Could it be Port La Forêt?

Δ Day 10

"That's enough guff," the president of the Atlantic Residents Association declared. He said he was fed up of his skipper's gibberish.

"No more updates or logs," he shouted.

"It must be that Marion woman editor you're feedin' to fill her desires."

"Sure were the residents not already clogging up the ship's computer and would they not be better writing Christmas cards or letters to Santy?"

The skipper agreed.

So, logs and updates are down by decree of the president. We now send a 'blog' for James Boyd and help save his sat phone bill. By the way, Neil O'Hagan of the Atlantic Youth Trust nearly drowned in his tears when he got a bill of 250 dollars for one call to the residents.

Last night was another howler. At one stage I registered 46 knots and again, alone in the black night, I was on the edge. I formally dressed up in my oils and went on deck to drop all sail. Then a massive wave struck. It overpowered Molly Malone, our self-steering system, for a crash gybe as all hell broke loose. This was real mast-breaker stuff.

The main locked against the runner, the keel was the wrong way and she lay on her side. Like falling off a 14-foot wall, I crashed down from the high side and ended up with my feet in the water at the aft quarter and luckily, a guard rail, saved me from eternity. I momentarily saw eternity before my eyes — but the good Lord decided I could have another few days in Paradise.

I struggled up, released the runner and the sheets and cantered the keel allowing the boat to become upright and normalised. We rode out the storm, like John Wayne might, and headed off into the dawn.

Early morning, we turned the corner, so-to-speak, passing just inside Flores, the most western of the Azores islands and Horta. They are beautiful islands. It looks like we might have missed the party with three other IMOCA 60s stopping there.

The Azores were like a gate we passed through, leaving behind a miserable grey few days. Daylight brought bright sunlight. It glistened and jumped off the wave tops and blue seas. It was no longer James Joyce's snotgreen. It blew 25 knot winds and made for some powerful sailing. The little bit of warmth, as I peeled layers off, was only vainglorious. The Atlantic Residents Association had a great day out. With many boats out of the race, and fewer on the ocean bed, the skipper had less pressure to perform.

Other than that folks, not much else to report and perhaps a toast, learned from Sean Lemass:

To the Lady Nicola:

'To the Ship that Goes
To the Wind that Blows
...And the Lass who loves a sailor..'

And with that, tomorrow I will share my wisdom with young sailors and reveal my great secret to good navigation.

Δ Day 11

As promised from yesterday, I can now disclose the great secret. It was given to me by an old Master Mariner, Captain Wholley, in the Galway sea scouts as a child.

"Me boy," says he.

"The secret to all good navigation is to steer around the rocks."

That advice is a metaphor for life itself.

The only rocks I had to steer around, after leaving St Barts, were the Azores; next are the ones at the 'Ferretland' finish.

And that's it: my reason for having survived, so far.

Meanwhile, all is well after an uneventful day on Currency House Kilcullen. I did practice my trumpet again.

The wind keeps honking at 30 knots-plus and we keep surfing over, under and through the majestic Atlantic rolling waves maintained so well by the Atlantic Residents Association.

Through Night and Day
Through Wind and Storm
Through Hail and Fog
Remember the Great Secret
Happy Christmas

¶ ¶ ¶ ¶

And that was my last log entry. In a battered state with blown-out headsails and just a storm jib and a badly damaged main, I made it across the finish line on a sharp sunny cold day on the 20th December off the coast of Brittany.

I had to pinch myself.

Was this for real?

Right up to the finish line I was totally on the edge.

And then a massive release.

I was third over the line to take a podium position.

It was staggering; unbelievable.

It was totally unexpected. I had proved wrong those who said I would never do it. And to gain a placing was the icing on the cake.

What a Christmas present. I was up there with the professional sailors.

I had become a pro at least in name, since the sponsor never came up with the promised funds to cover the costs.

At the prize-giving ceremony in the full auditorium the three winning skippers were on stage being interviewed. The MC asked what they did to manage their sleep patterns and what training and preparations they adhered to.

As true professionals the others explained, giving examples of going to the hospital, meeting with the doctors, putting sleep sensors on their brains and working out optimum times, how to manage and so forth.

And then it was my turn.

I could clearly see the audience, at that stage, was beginning to get bored. They wanted the formal part to end and the party to begin.

So I was silent for a moment before: "Oh, I had a pint of Guinness each day to prepare." With that the auditorium erupted in laughter. The Irishman had become a caricature of himself, and happily found his way home for Christmas.

LESSONS FROM CHAPTER 6
- ↗ If you don't ask, you don't get.
- ↗ By getting to the line, by starting and staying the course, you might be amazed by your success.
- ↗ Be careful with whom you set out to sail the Atlantic.

Chapter 7

Sponsored Journeys

EVEN though I had qualified to start the Vendée, I had still not made the final commitment in public. Though I would not have admitted it at the time, in my heart of hearts, this was my destiny, my dream and my focus. Whether it was the Volvo around the World Race, the Vendée or other adventures, getting sponsorship and funding the projects — amazing as they may be — was an extraordinary challenge and learning experience.

While I had been able to afford the boat, the running costs at high professional level are enormous. I had to raise sponsorship

Getting backing is an adventure. It's tough in a sport that some consider to be on the margins.

My quest for sponsorship did not start or finish with the Vendée. It included seeking sponsorship for the Whitbread Around the World Race, then the Volvo race and many more projects in between, both on my own account and for others. It ranged from time spent in Tokyo, being detained by corporate security in Bonn, to accusations of corporate espionage and getting an executive fired. Here is a flavour of some of my adventures.

¶ ¶ ¶ ¶

Dreams, such as we had, cost money and involve risk. I was ready. While well established in other markets and in particular France, Ireland simply had few corporates who could justify the budget. And even fewer with the marketing creative, flair and understanding — in particular how to use something like this. I would even go further to say that many so-called marketeers are brain dead.

In one case I offered title sponsorship at no cost and perhaps a contribution high KPIs (Key Performance Indicators) if they got some value. And they still did not get it.

From my Transatlantic Race when my sponsor did not come up with the money, I have learned a lot the hard way.

Being truthful, I would rather not have learned as much.

But come join me on the sponsorship journeys; the ones where it really was necessary to push the boundaries. Not just for my own global circumnavigation but several other projects, in which I was successful in raising funding, either on my own or with others. Some were commercial; most were simply loves, passions and charities undertaken on a voluntary basis because they were needed.

¶ ¶ ¶ ¶

Selling sponsorship is tough. The decision process is still a black art despite the science of data analytics and more precise evaluation of return on investment. But no matter how hard people try to evaluate it by numbers, much of it remains subjective.

The old adage that 'half the money you spend on adverting is wasted but no one knows which half' is replicated in sponsorship, only it's even harder to quantify.

To derive value from sponsorship, the personal interest of the decision-making executives is vital. Apart from their understanding, it becomes a passion and interest outside the job for which they are paid. The real professionals and leaders will drive whatever they take on with a passion, regardless.

But it is an added challenge when you're attempting to sell multi-million euro sponsorships in a sport many would not consider mainstream.

Mix that in with timelines, big corporates and tales of the unexpected and you get an idea of the extraordinary dimensions it can take on.

What follows are some bizarre experiences I had with Japanese, German and Chinese companies. Many of the 'wins' were part of a team undertaking in which I played a role. Others were my solo runs that spanned from the sublime to the ridiculous.

Like much in life, great failures are often more interesting than successful ones. Indeed my quests and stubborn determination led to one senior executive, based in Brussels in the Bridgestone Japanese company, getting fired. He was not happy at all with me at the time, but had the grace some time later to admit it had been a good thing.

On a different project it led to another senior executive in the German company, DHL, also being fired after a Gestapo-like investigation. Thankfully he was reinstated later too. I had to work overtime to take the blame and save him.

We also had Chinese executives wrestling with loss of face, locking our skipper Ian Walker in a room with no bathroom so that he had to pee in the plant pots.

I was embarrassed by many escapades and I write about them with some reluctance. But, having said that, they were extraordinary examples of 'Gorilla Sales'. I think they stand out as sagas worth telling because we can all learn from them.

The Bridgestone Story

Des Collins has thanked me since but not when my actions led to him being sacked from Japanese tyre-maker Bridgestone. Based in Brussels, Irishman Des had worked his way to a senior executive position. When he got the sack he was, understandably, highly upset with me.

Since being fired, Des has written a successful book called 'Sushi and Fries'. It outlined his time and experiences working as a European employee of what many consider a great Japanese company.

But it could also be described as having a glass ceiling for non-Japanese in the company.

Glass ceilings are generally used to denote difficulty for women to be promoted to senior management positions. The phenomenon was highlighted by Ann Morrison in her book "Breaking the Glass Ceiling" from her work at the Centre for Creative Leadership in San Diego, California.

This is an organisation I have worked with and admire. In my view, real leadership is about risk taking. But it should be risk we need to understand and calculate — as I have highlighted earlier.

In his book, Des explains his glass ceiling (though he does not use that term). He explains how cultural differences can lead to conflict and misunderstanding between Asians and Europeans.

He says: "Nowhere is this more evident than in the overseas subsidiary of a Japanese corporation." Bizarrely I stumbled into this in what was a curious adventure (which, in the end, led nowhere) that cost a lot of time and money.

In 'Sushi and Fries,' Des also deals with the obstacles that Japanese managers face when they are assigned to Europe.

While in one way these glass ceilings can protect companies and societies, in many others they do a great deal of damage. They can frustrate and hold back talent and progress.

The first big step to understanding any such phenomenon is to recognise it is there. But doing something about it, or navigating around it, is another matter entirely.

Using real-life stories from his 30 years experience working for Bridgestone, Des shared his adventures. Some are funny, some tragic, but all are honest examples of what happens behind the doors of this Fortune 500 corporation with its roots firmly in Asia.

He was one of a tiny number of Europeans who reached the position of vice-president.

So, from his vantage point he could observe the conflicts and confusion which regularly block business development and choke creativity and inspiration.

Des suggests solutions to the difficulties faced by Japanese managers and their European employees. He tries to inspire a better working environment for both. Unlike other books that merely describe official Japanese business practices, it tells real stories from real situations — and the consequences of them.

My story was only one example.

As a case in point, Bridgestone was transformed after 14 years as a partner in Formula 1 motor racing globally. It changed the company. Des explained how withdrawal from Formula 1 became an even bigger challenge after a change of HQ management.

There was massive loss of market share. Des described how handling personnel differed for Japanese employees and non-Japanese employees. In essence it underlines why foreign companies will always be foreign.

I was encouraged by Des, who could see the value in supporting a team in the Volvo Ocean Race. There would also be value for Bridgestone to have the opportunity to collaborate with Volvo, one of the world's largest tyre buyers (between their truck, car, bus and other companies in the auto sector).

While responsible for Europe, he needed the global marketing specialists and senior management to buy in from Japan. That was my foot-in-the-door. Or so I thought.

Hot to trot, and hungry to get myself in front of the decision makers, I bought a ticket to Tokyo. I also paid a professional agency a lot of money to prepare a 'pitch-book' for Bridgestone. It was surreal landing into this business culture as a non-Japanese.

Unbeknownst to me when I arrived, the management had decided this project was not for them. They had already communicated that to Europe. But, of course, I didn't know. No wonder they were totally surprised when I showed-up in a sharp suit, polished shoes and cufflinks.

And so a room full of Japanese executives met me, perhaps out of politeness or curiosity or simply not wishing for anyone to lose face.

I learned later they were fuming and the organisation was mad with Des. But nobody told me this (or more likely I did not listen properly). It had been incorrectly interpreted that Des had gone against their wishes and encouraged me to go to Japan anyway. That was not the case.

To me this was harmless: just an airline ticket and an adventure for a keen dude who could see the value of our proposition for sponsorship. Okay, they said 'No'. So be it. That was their right. To get the business you have to try: to ask the question and to meet the people. So what if I blew the travel costs and work time on a wild goose chase? It was not at someone else's expense.

I learned later it was the final straw for Des and a reason they fired him. My fault: a senior executive in his prime now unemployed, with a family to look after.

Subsequently he wrote the book which sold well. He was hired by Continental, another company in the tyre industry and I understand he has been extremely happy since.

The DHL story

The goal was to raise €16m in sponsorship — the price of a winning campaign in the Volvo Ocean Race. So I set about finding it with increased energy.

By my contrary way of seeing things, being rejected only drove me to try harder.

It was no longer the objective to just complete the course; now it was to win. That's why I concluded we needed, at least, that type and scale of sponsorship. I had managed to learn to think big. That's what coming from a West of Ireland small community can do for you. We are only limited by our imaginations.

DHL (Deutsche Post), the massive courier and financial services company had caught my attention due to its growing global nature and ambitions. It was also a service used by business and attached to what the marketers called an AB1: senior level, high income executives and decision makers.

The journey to making a €40 billion company (400 x €100m companies) had a twin-pronged starting point. One was a dynamic courier company founded as DHL in Australia. It had a fast-moving can-do Aussie culture. The other was Deutsche Post, a state owned cumbersome institution which ran the country's postal service. It also had a powerful bank awash with cash.

The catalyst was Klaus Peter Richard Otto Zumwinkel. Klaus was a dynamic leader who started his career as a consultant with blue-chip business-advisory firm McKinsey. He was chief executive officer and chairman of Deutsche Post between 1990 and 2008. Then dramatically, under suspicion of tax fraud, he resigned on February 15, 2008.

He was convicted in January 2009, given a suspended sentence of two years imprisonment and fined one million euro.

But I am getting a little ahead of myself.

Let me start at the start.

I met him, when he was at the height of his powers, after I gate-crashed his party in the spectacular Hotel Petersburg overlooking Bonn, the former West German capital.

It was the same venue where Michael Schumacher, also at the height of his powers, got married and one which fired the imagination of the German public.

I figured out the inner operations of the company through a research project that, I believe, would have been the pride and joy of any private investigator or corporate espionage agent.

All my training in sales and management had taught me to figure out the 'decision matrix' of the company into which you are selling. It can be particularly complex in large companies with big contracts.

I made friends with the Czech Republic country manager and a senior executive charged with developing a major IT centre based in Prague.

This was a route into a company undergoing rapid transformation at top level. I also befriended the DHL chief executive officer for the Australia and New Zealand region. He was subsequently appointed to run the Australasian arm — one of four global regions into which the company was divided.

He was really enthusiastic about my concept. He could immediately see how he could use a global racing campaign to promote his business and use it as a unifying force both internally and on a global scale.

He said he could deliver 25 per cent of the budget — €4m — from his region.

But he explained the key was to get the global marketing head behind it and win the support of other regions.

That was a great start and a real foot-in-the-door.

Alongside all this was the fact that the DHL Deutsche Post company was growing at an exponential rate. As the old German Post office that had acquired the DHL courier company it was a simple, clutter free and dynamic brand.

This was a really good time to get inside the head of the conglomerate, build relationships and start a successful long-term sponsorship. It could be a win-win for all.

The speed of change and growth in a company can be gauged by the example of my brother-in-law Martin McDonnell. He worked in transport and logistics all his life. He was the financial controller of a company acquired by a larger one. Not long afterwards the acquiring company was taken over by DHL/Deutsche Post. One can only begin to imagine the amount of activity involved on a global basis.

No better man than Martin. Yet even he had difficulty keeping up with the pace of takeovers, acquisitions and coming to grips with different cultures.

This was all happening and being driven by the brilliant Dr Zumwinkel. With ruthless German efficiency, I might add. No wonder it became a €40bn company with all the savings and pensions of German workers to play with.

Anyway, to move the project along I was advised to go to Bonn and informally meet the key executives on the fringe of an imminent global conference of the company's top 150 executives.

With more than 100,000 employees worldwide, this was a unique group, and the first conference of its kind.

It just so happened I had a planned holiday in Florida around that time. We were staying in Miami beach with my then partner, Lucie Bukova, and expecting our son, Cormac.

Little did he (now a teenager making his way in the world) know what his future dad was up to — let alone his mum.

Here's how things unfolded.

My Czech DHL manager contact sent me the schedule for the global conference and the participants. I found out later the schedule was top secret and he should not have circulated it.

Meanwhile, we had just three days left before we were due to fly back to Prague from our Florida holiday.

The meeting was highly confidential with major global strategic issues and company secrets to be discussed.

Needless to say, the company secrets didn't matter a hoot to me. My sole objective was to win a global sponsorship deal and a €16m sale.

So with the prospect of getting close to the decision makers I changed my ticket, headed for Miami airport and connected to Bonn.

That meant Lucie was left behind to fly directly to Prague and enjoy — or so we hoped — the last few days on the beach.

To drag her body through flight connections to Bonn in her current state was not the best idea in the world. Mind you, the fact that her credit card would not work when I left complicated matters somewhat. As you can guess, the fact she subsequently ran out of money, on her own in a strange land, piled on the problems.

And little did I know what was to unfold for me as, blindly and innocently, I set out for Germany.

I had few clothes. I was travelling light in shorts. After balmy Florida, northern European weather was a cold reminder that it was only April. It hit me hard when I landed in Bonn. In the taxi, in a city I had never been and knew little about, I made friends with the driver.

With a great command of English and fascinated by the mission I shared with him, he guided me to a gentleman's outfitters to buy a business suit, shoes, shirt, and tie. It was a transformation. Complete with cufflinks and polished shoes, I changed to looking like a real executive with a tan. Yes, I felt I had the appearance of a man ready to do a €16m deal.

The master plan was to hang out at the DHL Bonn headquarters and socialise in the hotels, pubs and restaurants with the visiting executives.

That was my advice from my new DHL executive friend. The idea was to infiltrate the organisation, find and build relationships with the decision makers. I felt it was a good way to do things in a company that had expanded so fast. I surmised the right hand might not be quite sure of what the left was up to.

DHL Deutsche Post was well known in Bonn as a large and powerful corporate animal. Their massive glass skyscraper was an institution and landmark. It had formerly been occupied by the federal government which had relocated to Berlin. And Klaus Zumwinkel, with his immense spending power, was the corporate equivalent of God on Earth at the height of his power.

This was also the first time English was the working language of the worldwide meeting. It was a mark of the company's true globalisation. There was an air of excitement around the reception area in the conference hotel. Shirted, suited, polished and shaved, I mixed in with the executives and joined the coach taking them the short trip to the corporate HQ.

I learned afterwards the company had intensive private security that was German in its intimidating efficiency. Being an old institution with a civil service mentality, there was little trust.

However, for that historic senior level global executive meeting — with people representing new bolt-on acquisitions — there was an extra effort to be seen to be casual and informal. The drive was to change the culture from being rigid, structured and institutionalised — like the old German state post office company — to a relaxed US-style outfit.

To land in the middle of this was fascinating, regardless of any sponsorship deal plan. I joined the energy of the gathering.

With my executive suit and suntan I fitted right in and flowed with the other executives to the inner-sanctum meeting hall.

I could not believe my luck.

I was enjoying the corporate presentations as if I was one of them. Like weddings we had gate-crashed as students, each side thought I was with the other; so I had free rein.

As well as that, of course, in Bonn I was coming from my journalistic background too so it was not unusual to be invited to, and participate in, corporate events. The fact that many of the discussions at this particular gig were highly sensitive and confidential within the company went totally over my head.

Truth be told, I couldn't have given a damn. The internal police didn't know that, as I was to learn later.

I was intense. I had been building relationships with the key people running the business in different parts of the world. Many had not met each other.

From earlier contact, the progressive Australian CEO had indicated he could find €4m. So it was a matter of pulling together each of the other regions.

It was all about figuring out the decision matrix. I had learned this from my corporate training in 'big-ticket' sales. Get to the decision makers.

So the day progressed. I started to feel like one of that elite group; even more so in the evening as we gathered at the Hotel Petersburg, a large and lavish castle complex overlooking Bonn.

It was an incredible event. Budget was no object. It was all done to generate energy, excellence and reflect the power of Herr Zumwinkel.

He was exuding power. I could feel it with, and around, him as we shook hands. The event was designed to filter energy and power through the company.

Even though I had been advised to meet on the fringes, I had worked my way into the inner circle. Indeed, at one stage I ended up in conversation with Herr Zumwinkel. He came across as a lovely, charismatic man.

Meanwhile, back in Florida, I had a big problem. Lucie Bukova, then expecting our son Cormac, was stranded. I had cut short my holiday with her on Miami Beach to follow the DHL opportunity in Germany and left her to fly back to Prague on her own, as planned.

Unfortunately the credit card would not work. She had no cash and she was stuck sorting the final payment for accommodation and cash to get to the airport and so forth. Finally, with multiple phone calls and payment transfers, it got sorted.

Between meeting 'fellow' executives and working the crowd in Bonn, I was on my mobile (a then cumbersome 'Nokia Brick') a lot.

My heavy phone use attracted attention from the 'discreet' security service. I was to learn later I'd added great excitement to their lives. And one of the DHL top marketing corporate executives became suspicious. Being afraid to probe and risk causing upset to a possible 'colleague' he tipped off security about my suspicious behaviour.

It all came to a head at the conference the following morning. The security men had convinced themselves their protective shield had been breached and that they had discovered someone committing corporate espionage. They pounced. Four armed guards arrived from different directions and I was hauled away.

I was held in detention and suddenly frightened. The private police were orgasmic. Finding people like me (or what they thought I was) meant concrete justification for their existence.

It didn't matter to them that they'd acted beyond their powers (my hotel room was raided).

Without consent or legal entitlement, they took my laptop and 'Brick' phone. Their data mining had begun. By God, my computer and emails must have confused them: Florida, Czech Republic, Ireland etc.

The conference was over by lunchtime. The various executives headed off back to their corners of the world.

But the Czech executive who had given me the programme for the conference was promptly taken off his train and rushed back to Bonn for interrogation. He was immediately suspended.

Me? At first, in total isolation, I would not talk. Or should I say I was economical with the truth. I did not wish to betray my sources. This only served to compound the mystery.

Until eventually the penny dropped.

The serious nature of my situation became blindingly apparent. The only sensible thing to do was tell them everything.

The full truth.

The thing was, it was a problem for the security people. They were convinced they had picked up on someone in a case of real corporate espionage.

It was hard for them to accept I was a simple Irishman seeking a sponsor, for no commercial gain, so that my home town could have a team in the Volvo Ocean Race.

It was, I told them, something I was working on voluntarily with no prospect of commercial gain.

These private corporate security people had acted beyond their powers, as I've said. They had arrested me privately, threatened me and interrogated me intensely.

But eventually, while they had great difficulty understanding me (both in substance and language) they realised I was telling the truth and was not part of some industrial conspiracy.

I was eventually released the following day. But not before signing every sort of form you could imagine — from confidentiality to admission of guilt and undertaking not to disclose anything discussed at the conference.

Needless to say I missed my flight back to Prague.

It was some time before I got my phone and computer back. And for several weeks afterwards I became aware that my phones were being tapped and monitored.

Fortunately too the executive who had helped me, all out of goodwill, was reinstated. Merely as a by-the-way, the chief executive officer and chairman of Deutsche Post resigned some time later. It had nothing to do with me, I might add, but he was convicted in January 2009 for tax fraud, given a two-year suspended sentence and fined one million euro.

And no, in case you were wondering, DHL did not sponsor us in the Volvo.

But the Chinese did. Here's the how and wherefore of that adventure.

The Chinese deal

For the 2008/2009 Around the World Race, we managed to secure a historic and unprecedented Chinese sponsorship commitment.

It was for our Around the World team and for hosting the Volvo Ocean Race in Galway.

Jamie Boag led our team and organisation and we were supported by Volvo. We also secured major support (€8m) from the Irish government. Our overall budget was €21m. That is a massive undertaking for any start-up group whose leadership was on a totally voluntary community basis.

Even if I do say so myself, it was an incredible success.

If viewed in the context of a once-off, the unprecedented amount from government was extraordinary.

It did not happen by accident; ultimately it was driven by the powerful logic of the business case and the return it would generate.

At a time of economic crisis, expenditure on tourism brings a much quicker return.

It was also great fun, an amazing adventure. I was proud to be involved. It reconnected me in a wonderful way with my home town. Sponsors got a great payback for Galway alone: the event attracted more than 600,000 visitors. According to an independent study, the direct benefit to the local and national economy was estimated to be in excess of €100m.

We had formed an umbrella group called 'Let's Do It Global'.

I was the founding chairman and put the professional corporate structure in place.

Most important was openness, transparency and proper controls to run the project professionally.

Within this framework, we had 'Let's Do It Green' led by Eamon Conneely who was responsible for the boat and 'Let's Do It Galway' led by John Killeen with responsibility for the port. Collectively we were dubbed The Three Amigos.

In the name 'Let's Do it Green' there were equal connotations of friendliness, environment or, in another context, Ireland. The name gave us a broader base in our global quest to get sponsorship.

A condition of hosting the race in Galway was that we put a team in the Volvo Ocean Race Around the World. It was an incredible adventure; what we did was unprecedented.

We repeated the event in 2012. This too went incredibly well and attracted the same numbers and brought great economic benefits.

However, as a race finish and not a long-stopover, it was not as dynamic. The weather was also not as kind — but that's an inherent risk with outdoor events and success is planned, regardless of the weather.

The event itself and the business benefit to Galway and Ireland (tax take) made the undertaking a success. The awful part, though, was that we ended up with a financial shortfall that second time.

The government agency Fáilte Ireland that we dealt with did not cover itself in glory; nor did the then management of the Volvo Ocean Race who exploited our situation.

The overrun was small relative to the benefit and turnover but it was tough and we suffered. The alternative was to let it fail and do even more damage as well as giving satisfaction to the hurlers on the ditch.

The naysayers had their time.

The newspaper headlines gave us grief, as did social media clatter, guff and whatever you're having yourself.

It's simply human nature to gloat about other people's failures. Or what they consider that to be.

Failure is the naked and raw underbelly of risk. And we all remember the failures. Such is life. It's one of the great things about small communities in Ireland: we keep each other in our place — call it 'tall poppy' syndrome.

It is the other extreme in the United States. Enterprise is driven in a massively positive way. Ask the average American how they are and they (most likely) say: "I'm just great — and how about you?" Donald Trump set out to "make America great again".

If you ask someone how they are in Ireland, the most likely response is: "Ah! sure, I'm not too bad."

Being honest (don't you love that expression we have? It's as if to imply we're not normally honest) I like small communities because they keep us all in our place and don't let us lose contact with reality or rise above our station.

But back to hosting the Volvo Ocean Race and the cost over-runs. . .

It all had a happy ending. It took more than three years to resolve, with virtually every outstanding bill settled and terms negotiated. Most were reasonable when the situation was explained. It was not easy in the middle of a major economic downturn. Again we did it for no personal benefit, but the satisfaction, sense of community and being in a position to give something back made it worthwhile.

Many helped. But John Killeen, my other principal partner (who gave enormous time, leadership and vision for no personal gain) and I agreed we should acknowledge Declan Dooley the accomplished publisher and former President of Galway Chamber of Commerce. He wore the same chain of office once worn by my late father.

Of course, when it was all resolved and the entire project finally put to bed, there were no headlines, no interviews and no social media clatter — in complete contrast to what had gone before.

Most important for us all was that it brought closure. For those who cared to find out, our personal reputations for delivering and doing what we promised remained intact. Even more importantly, for those who take on such a project again, previous success showed it can be done.

As was to be the case with my subsequent nightmare of losing a mast, it is the great disasters that people selectively remember — not the fact that I went back, rebuilt and completed the circumnavigation.

That is the simple reality of life.

Ultimately it is what you do, not what you fail to do, that matters.

Or does it?

LESSONS FROM CHAPTER 7
- ↗ Cultural differences in large global companies vary massively. To be successful you must understand this.
- ↗ Fundamentals do not change. People relate and connect with people, no matter what culture, background or nationality they come from.

- ↗ Not losing face is a fundamental part of Chinese culture and thinking — to the point where its loss, or potential loss, is actually written into contracts.
- ↗ In seeking sponsorship, like much in life, great failures are often more interesting than successful ones.
- ↗ Real leadership is about risk taking. But it should be a risk we understand and calculate.
- ↗ It is what you do, not what you fail to do, that matters.

Chapter 8
The Start

LEAVING sponsorship journeys to one side and being fortunate I had been able to fund this latest campaign without sponsorship, the time had come for me to start the Vendée and fulfil my dream.

During the race build-up I felt at times like a goldfish in a bowl. The world was looking in and I was swimming around in plain view: helpless, hapless and exploding to be released onto the open ocean.

To be on the Vendée Globe Racing was utterly amazing. It was an emotional roller-coaster and the culmination of a lifetime's work, preparation and drive. In short, I had earned it and if I was spending my children's inheritance, so be it ... although hopefully I would have enough left.

I had arrived three weeks before the gun on the Kilcullen Voyager in Le Sables d'Olonne. It was to do what I had set out to do.

My time had come.

The dream was ready to become reality.

A scary reality at that.

My personal journey to the edge was just beginning.

Sailing solo on the ocean breaks all the rules when it comes to keeping a watch at sea.

No matter who you are, or what it is, we all need a challenge.

There were three informal categories of skipper. These are:
▶ The top professionals on multi-million euro budgets;
▶ The 'wannabe professionals';
▶ The dreamers.

And while fanciful to be a serious contender, I was in the latter category. Each of 29 teams who started out of 30 qualifiers was led by determined individuals. They had extraordinary stories to tell in the complex, demanding (physically and emotionally) scramble to get to the start-line. The whole thing was surreal.

I constantly asked myself: "Is this real?"

Looking back now, it was all like being in a trance. Some 400,000 people were said to have lined the long harbour pier and route from our berth to the start line and the open ocean.

It is an ocean runway that makes Les Sables famous.

In the build-up, an estimated 2,500,000 people visited the Race Village. As it only takes place every four years, it is a massive commercial event; rows and rows of tents, exhibits, sponsor promotions, corporate hospitality etc.

It was an amazing honour and privilege to have so many interested in what was in the end a personal quest and, dare I say, a selfish target.

The contrast between massive attention, tensions, excitement, large crowds, hype and downright fear to being totally alone on the ocean could not have been greater.

I could feel the power of the crowd pushing me on. Some would revel in the prospect of disaster and others in the prospect of success. All were plugged into the prospect of trying.

And suddenly, after emotional goodbyes, I was alone.

Oh yes, one thing. I had kept a painful shoulder injury to myself. More anon.

One of the rules of the race as I indicated earlier was that every skipper should send photo, video and written logs back to race headquarters on a regular basis. From a commercial viewpoint this is now necessary for sponsors as it brings many people 'with you' on the journey.

Looking back, it was great to have these logs to reflect on. It was also a discipline. With so much to do constantly on the boat, the duty may not have been fulfilled if it wasn't compulsory.

Δ Log 2, Day 2

Bonjour. Here I am, 2nd day at sea, contemplating the world and reflecting on the wonderful send-off from my Lady Nicola, family and friends who travelled to Les Sables. It was magic. The Vendée race organisers and all in Les Sables deserve a lot of credit. As do the Kilcullen core team: Simon, David, Hammy, Gilda, Mr Perfect, Neil and Bosman Marcus.

All of a sudden I have been transported from guff and pre-race frenzy to being totally alone.

The start buzz included chatting with Prince Albert of Monaco, patron of the race, about his late mum Princess Grace. Alongside was my own princess daughter, Aisling. She danced a jig on my boat deck for Albert and on live TV, as we cast off with the Unthinkable Bodhran Player (your skipper) supported by Cormac and Mícheál from Innishear who travelled for the start.

As did many supporters such as David Beattie, Peter Cooke, my sisters Pauline with Ken, and Annmarie with Peter, to mention just a few.

Now it's total isolation here in the dark, in busy shipping lanes off Cape Finisterre.

It was like somebody waved a magic wand and the spell has me here, huddled over a navigation table. Like the cockpit of a spacecraft where I am destined to spend the next 100 days. By then hopefully my shoulder and knees will have recovered from being thrown over the handlebars of a bike in the race village.

While painful, it's not stopping me from running the boat; and those spinlock knee-pads I picked up are mighty.

¶ ¶ ¶ ¶

My start was a disaster. In my eagerness, I was early over the line. The choice was to get a 5-hour penalty or go back and risk the zillions of spectator boats.

There is no excuse. I should have known better. I lost about 90 minutes and had a near-collision with a spectator boat. They say the photos were good. In the context of the race now, it hardly matters.

It has been a grand idea, a brilliant event and getting to the start line an achievement in itself. But now I don't know. What in hell's name have I done?

I have no idea what lies ahead. What in the name of humanity have I let myself in for?

Though the first night at sea was cold and miserable, at least it's starting to warm up as we move south.

Let's see.

¶ ¶ ¶ ¶

I need to tell you about that shoulder injury. During those first few days at sea, I was suffering badly from a bike accident prior to the start.

Cycling is one of my great joys. I loved the freedom of riding around the Race Village and cycling from our team accommodation to the boat.

It was early morning. I was cycling down the village entrance. The area was empty. Suddenly, without warning, a delivery van reversed out and I whacked straight into it, head over heels. I damaged my shoulder in the process. Fortunately there was nothing broken; just a massive strain. After getting medical help, I kept the injury to myself as far as possible.

I was afraid it might stop me starting. Nothing would hold me back but it was painful and an extra struggle. Luckily, it is a different muscle set to the ones needed for winding the winches on board.

Those few pre-race weeks were like a whirlwind. I was never as well prepared for sailing. All the hard lessons previously learned were executed. Each day the team would meet and review the worklist under the superb overall guidance of Marcus Hutchinson.

This involved making a meal bag for each day, thinking through almost every possibility, double checking everything and loading the boat with spare parts.

Though solo, it was a massive team effort.

And each day the pressure was building.

The night before I left, we spent time with friends and family at Le Galway Irish Pub. Among those there were Minister Simon Coveney and many Irish and French friends.

Many, led by Sheena Kelleher, came from the locally-based Irish community in Les Sables.

Δ Day 3

'I know a man who knew a man who ate an elephant.' Or so the story goes. The way he did it was a little bit at a time and he had his life to do it.

Now off the coast of Portugal, I have 100 days to eat my elephant — after that I run out of food. I cannot imagine what Sir Robin Knox-Johnston was like after almost 310 days at sea when he completed the first Golden Globe solo in 1968.

I would not admit it at first, but I was seasick; in a heap, cold and miserable the first night. However, I have learned to manage it. Emotional intelligence they call it — and I am now completely over it.

Perhaps it was just a pent-up consequence of last week. Who knows?

We made up for it with some glorious sailing down the coast of Portugal today. The joy, excitement and positives from the French community were amazing and a delightful escape in these days of terrorism threats and economic challenges.

And did I mention the Hilary and Donald show?

Back on board: no moon has surfaced. It's black outside. Wind speed is 17.8 knots and we're doing 13.6 knots almost fully upwind on target to clear the TSS Zone off Lisbon, 60 miles south. My big worry is a collision. I have four ships on the AIS within five miles but it's the rogue unmarked vessels and odd fishing boats that scare me. Also you simply never know what you might hit. The chances are less on the deep ocean so I can't wait to get out there.

Most of the rest of the fleet have opted to go further west out to sea and they're a bit faster. My hope is to make as much direct southing first and within another 250 miles to pick up the first North Easterly Trade winds before the others and catch up a little. There is not much to lose at this point, so it's worth a try.

¶ ¶ ¶ ¶

Day 4 was cancelled. No Log. I was sad and almost depressed. Trump was elected, much to my horror. I was also struggling with the boat and the ocean. As well as that the fleet was getting away from me.

Reefs in, reefs out, sails up, sails down — all hard work.

I was sad. Like I had the weight of the world on my shoulders, there I was in the middle of the ocean. Helpless.

¶ ¶ ¶ ¶

Δ Day 5

Now what a difference a day makes.

Trump may not be so bad.

Our strategy of staying east to pick up the North Easterly trades a little sooner, or at least at the same time as the others, seems to be working. At least we're back in touch. The bright full moon beams are dancing in the dark as we power south towards the Canary Islands.

Here in the darkness, I am punching out this diary crouched on the nav table. We picked up the trades around midday and were soon honking at boat speeds of 17 and 19 knots in 23 knot winds.

Champagne sailing.

I am also becoming more in tune with the boat, though today did have its hairy moment. I got immersed, soaked to the skin, when submerged by an enormous wave on the foredeck taking the J3 over the side. It took a long time to sort it all out. Every single day on deck I think of my friend Willie who we lost overboard in the Southern Ocean when a rope lifted him unexpectedly over. I will tell you more about that later.

Secured, I am getting used to thinking of President Trump — that's so-called democracy. Lots of small town middle-Americans have been crushed by free market and jobs exported so they have had their say. Rick Wilson, on Great America IV, is upset.

The world will survive and our next great adventure together could be walking the US-Mexican Wall.

Now the days start to roll by.

The first five were nothing; in other voyages that would be an eternity,

Another and another and another.

And still another sunrise.

The same yet different; different yet the same

¶ ¶ ¶ ¶

LESSONS FROM CHAPTER 8

↗ With highs, you can be sure lows will inevitably follow. The trick is how to manage both.

↗ A journey like this underlines the importance of not getting too far ahead of yourself... of staying in the moment.

Chapter 9
Atlantic Ocean

I WAS getting further out, deeper into the Atlantic and moved south past the Canary Islands. In retrospect, I should have held more to the west in accordance with conventional wisdom. However, both my shoulder injury and a personal interest in the islands brought me close.

I was falling behind in the overall race. That was depressing. My goal was to finish. Deep down, however, that competitive urge demanded I do better. Early runner in the fleet was my friend Alex Thomson of Hugo Boss who was blazing a trail in his light-weight foiling craft.

Δ Day 6

I'm constantly living on the edge as I surf down a wave at 19 knots in a gust, while punching out the log on this keyboard below deck. Lucky to be living.

Earlier off the Canaries we had 29-knot gusts and went dangerously close to a fishing boat. He had no AIS. Now it's dark and, while still close to the islands, I have all the deck lights on and the strop on top of the mast flashing. It's a bit early but we're like a Christmas tree. I just don't want to take any chances. Soon it will be safer in the deep ocean.

It's been a tough 24 hours. A sail would not foil properly so I opted to take it down and had to go the wrong side and it went into the water. It was a struggle to recover it alone.

Also, the second reef line broke and it will be a challenge to fix. To boot, the port hydro generator holding bolt came undone. I got it back on board before any damage was done. There is always something but that's the life on the ocean wave.

'My soul's in the salt of the sea
In the weight of the wave
In the bubbles of foam
In the ways of the wind'
(Joseph Plunkett)

Δ Day 9

No sign of the moon yet. We have 15 knots of wind and 12.4 knots of boat speed sailing at an angle of about 140. The sea has flattened out.

Upfront again, Alex Thomson seems to be pulling clear. I would love him to win. It's tough going leading against the top French pros who are consumed with the race. We joked a lot before the start, especially when I encountered Alex with his hairstylist before going sailing. He was seeking that perfect wave in his hair — for the fashion snaps.

Back here, we're happily moving along in a more leisurely fashion. We should be more competitive. I think my detour around the Canaries did not help; neither did the sail problems. Also, being away from the fleet, one possible explanation is that I have been sailing at slightly wider angles.

But now, sort of back in the hunt, I seem to be staying with the fast, relentless pace; 24-7 or, for others, 25-8. Let's see.

When the wind inevitably gets lighter, and as we make for the doldrums, I will hopefully get my largest sail, the A3, unravelled. I should be flying now. I keep reminding myself that to finish is to win and keep our schools programme moving forward with the Atlantic Youth Trust. But I am hungry for performance.

The next big decision is whether to take a course straight through the Cape Verde islands or gybe and go more west where the wind angles and the breeze could be a bit better. Since I will hit the island during the day, the scenic route may be more interesting.

In fact, you don't see much at sea (though a 4 x 4 metre object was spotted floating below the surface which I will watch for in so far as it is possible). I only see other craft on screen.

Now away from everything in warmer waters, heating as we move south, the sheer vastness of the ocean strikes me again..

Today was my first easy day — just sailing on one tack. No gybes, reefs or sail changes. Time to contemplate, read (thanks Nicola, the Kindle is brilliant). And my musical instruments await; no one can hear me practise, let alone ever play. Up the Unthinkable Bodhran player.

Δ Day 10

Powering south-east towards the Cape Verde islands, I have yet to hit the doldrums. With each degree south it's getting warmer — moving towards the equator — and the winds are getting lighter.

Happily, I am also now becoming at one with the boat, sailing better, less on edge. The clutter of preparations is gone and several small problems on board have been resolved. Our team did an excellent job of preparation.

At around 04:00 hours I got a small shock. I was napping and was awoken by a series of muffled bangs on the port side. I hopped up in the cockpit to investigate. The unusual bullet-like noise did not repeat itself. I found nothing and went back to sleep, wondering.

I can sleep in the constant noise as this machine trundles along. However, you develop an extra sense that becomes attuned to the movement and noises of the boat. You may be asleep but when something different happens you're awake.

It was later in the morning, in the midday sun, that I picked up a funny smell. It led me to several dead flying fish cooking on deck. They could only be the explanation for my early morning awakening: a shoal of them had launched a 'kamikaze attack'.

Close to the Cape Verde islands it was a good day for wild life. I enjoyed the company of a school of dolphins for some time and talked to them. They would gather closer especially when I went forward on the bow. I would make a loud pitch whistle and they seemed to respond by jumping more frequently; more of them joined the fun too. It was my lone primitive way of communicating with them, whether real or imagined.

Also, it seems I have a fatal attraction for islands. Now, rather than go to the west of the Verdes, like most of the vessels, I decided to go through the islands. I counted nine. They stretch 110 miles east-west and about 100 miles north-south.

In a bizarre way, my routing software took me right through the centre of the longest and narrowest island, St Nicolas. With a choice to gybe right or go more upwind left of the Lady, I took the latter course — leaving St Nicolas on my right. I always walk with my Lady Nicola on the right. It was a good decision; we picked up some funnelled wind through the passage and have now cleared the islands.

Δ Day 11

It has been a frustrating day with little or no wind. At one stage I did complete 360 degrees following the breeze around. Indeed, sometimes it's harder to sail in light airs than a storm. My poor big toe also got a wallop walking around in bare feet.

Clearly having a sore toe is not an issue; no sympathy required. It must rank as a first-world problem.

I would like to be closer to the fleet and feel a bit left behind. Sure, there have been some on-board issues, but not enough to explain the gap. Being realistic my simple ambition is to get around safely.

Albert Einstein is a man I admire. So much so I have not followed his rules. He defined 'criteria' for madness as repeating the same thing again and again and expecting a different outcome. By those criteria over the past week, I qualify. It must be my West of Ireland sense of the contrary. If black is white, for no other reason than just to be different, I'd set out to prove white is black.

All the advisers and conventional wisdom said get west for better wind conditions. Yet each time I went east. Contrary? For sure. So I'm at least a day behind where I should be. I have an Einstein book on board for the voyage where this 'madness' is highlighted. It's a personality trait that often lands us in trouble.

We live — but do we learn?

△ Day 12

Today there was a total change in the sky and ocean. It went from being overcast and stable to blue skies, then green ocean and turbulent squalls. Or, as James Joyce describes it in Ulysses:

"The snotgreen sea.

The scrotumtightening sea".

One such squall caught me off-guard with its viciousness and strength. It overpowered the self-steering and the boat broached on her side. The loads on the rig were enormous but forgiving; in releasing one sheet — by a near miss — it almost brought my hand with it. Every moment, every day there are risks. As a self-discipline, I keep forcing myself to stop, consider and think of my body first before jumping into anything. Being caught off guard is what gets you.

Anyway, such was the speed and severity of the squall with little warning, I reckoned there could be more damage done trying to get all sails down. I knew it would not last so I simply took the helm and drove off in front of it. For 15 or 20 minutes, it roared, the rain lashed and the boat zoomed downwind. It was a great exhilarating ride on the edge.

Eventually, like life itself, it ran out of steam. The wind dropped back to 10 knots from 30 knots. After that, for the entire day, it was up and down. And it kept changing direction to make for a demanding and physical day.

Happily, though it is warm, we seem to have exited the doldrums and, though now upwind, we constantly make ground south towards the Equator. The pace is unrelenting.

Δ Day 14

Crossing the Equator

Let King Neptune rule the oceans as the Kilcullen and all aboard prepare to cross the Equator. When I take delivery of my first granddaughter, I will ask the King to bless her when we meet on the line tomorrow.

Let the pensioners cast off their sticks and jump for joy in the streets. A new child has arrived to support them and make our world a better place. She is Féile Roisin. Congratulations to my daughter Roisin and husband Roger for delivering a sister for Arthur. My role has been zero, except, of course, introducing her to King Neptune. Roisin had been long overdue. It had not been easy. I understand mother and child are all well.

Here on the ocean, emotions become more concentrated and boxed as we work our way south over the Equator.

To be truthful, I am not sure I am quite ready to be a parent never mind a grandparent. Maybe when I return from this adventure I will qualify. We live in hope that it will always triumph over reality.

I was premature in thinking we were clear of the doldrums. On Day 13 we once again found ourselves becalmed for a few hours.

Then suddenly from nowhere a blustery small storm erupted from the north.

There was no warning. It lashed and dumped enough rain to fill Lough Corrib. We had 27-knot gusts. And then it was gone, as quickly as it came. The 10-knot south easterly returned. There was no trace whatsoever of the storm on the weather map from my satellite. Regardless we had handled it well as I become more at one with the boat: she's an animal that needs minding with her constant demands.

Now on Day 14, quietly beating upwind working south, getting warmer and warmer, I am still suffering from staying too far to the east. But I am slowly getting back on track with the main fleet and at least holding my own.

All going well, Day 15 will be Equator Day. Since time began, it seems that seafarers have been celebrating King Neptune in wacky and wonderful ways as they cross the Equator.

Δ Day 15

My biggest problem today was a loud 'pop' as we crossed the Equator.

With a 15-knot cooling wind, we powered across the imaginary line at more than 13 knots. 'Champagne sailing' you might say. However, in my enthusiasm, the cork popped clear of the Kilcullen, thus complicating matters in my 'first-world' problem of the day.

The master strategy was to place a note in the bottle with a request to King Neptune for safe passage. There would also be a €50 note as a sort of encouragement to whoever finds the bottle to make contact. There was to be another request to King Neptune for a safe voyage through life for Feile Roisin, my new grand daughter. At 12 pounds plus, she arrived with considerable aplomb, late into the world at the weekend.

We have enough boat building materials on board to find a way to seal the bottle. Who knows, in years to come, if it will show up somewhere.

On crossing the Equator, I immediately convened a meeting of the South Atlantic Residents Association.

With just one member, it was not difficult. However, in true Brendan Behan tradition, the first item on the agenda was 'the split' and whether a North Atlantic Residence Association member — no longer in residence — would be acceptable in the south.

It was series of conversations between himself, myself and the other self. Such is the way my mind entertains itself alone.

All this mental exercise was going on against a backdrop of hard physical work: taking reefs in, shaking them out and changing sails. That was as well as everything else necessary to keep this 60 footer moving 24 hours a day.

My adventure is also a geography class. Early in the morning we will be leaving the islands of Fernando De Noronha to starboard, some 500 miles off the Brazil coast.

That's where fellow competitor and Frenchman Bernard de Broc is moored. Sadly his hull is damaged and he withdrew, deciding not to risk the southern Ocean. Bernard was much talked about in France during a previous race. That was when his tongue somehow got cut. Helped by a doctor on the phone he managed to sew it back together again.

The islands comprise a UNESCO world nature reserve. You have to get special permission to go there. From pictures, the scenery and beaches look amazing. There is an abundance of turtle and other sea life. And an ideal climate. It's definitely a place for the bucket list visit for a weekend or even a year? Perhaps do a Robinson Crusoe on it?

It's black on deck.

No moon.

Now we head towards the north-west coast of Brazil and veer south. Each day is a little cooler than the previous.

You might say that via Brazil is a roundabout way to get to South Africa (the Cape of Good Hope is the next turning mark).

However, by gradually curving, the plan is to navigate around the south Atlantic high and dive south first to the southern Ocean as soon as possible to pick up the prevailing westerlies in the Roaring Forties, Howling Fifties and, for me, porridge for breakfast.

Δ Day 16/17

If you're not living on the edge, you're taking up too much space

After the Equator 'high' and a lively discussion with King Neptune, it has been upwind sailing these past two days. The wind should have been from the east, as for the earlier boats, and not south-east for the past two days. Happily it has now reverted.

My shoulder is getting gradually better though it still hurts. My only other medical issue, if you could call it that, are salt sores on my posterior from wet or damp clothes. A raid on the first-aid kit and some dry clothes are helping ease the discomfort.

Now romping along at almost 14 knots in 17-knot winds we have started to move again. Powering along in the black of night you simply never know what's next. I feel a bit like the saying: "If you're not living on the edge, you're taking up too much space."

It's sad that Vincent Riou on PRB, the only previous winner, has dropped out. He is one of three in the last week — all experienced skippers with good boats. So you never know. All I can do is to keep a level head, minimise risk and maintain the boat in good shape. The rest is chance.

Having left autumn, had summer, it's spring now as we move straight south along the Brazilian coast. While it is tempting to take the shortest straight line towards South Africa, conventional wisdom says stay west and position yourself between weather systems so get south as fast as possible to pick up the Roaring Forties. Then it's east for the next 15,000 miles.

△ Day 18

Another day of slow, but solid, progress south along the Brazilian coast. Gradually I am catching some boats after my detours during the first 14 days. At least we are holding our own and psychologically I am pacing myself. However, I am somewhat nervous of the southern ocean ahead.

The raid on the first-aid kit to solve the salt-sores issue with my humble posterior is having an effect. It's now comfortable to sit again at the nav station. Through the angled window the sky is alive with stars; there are few clouds and no moon.

Currently it is full main, J2 headsail, 10.2 knots of wind speed, 11.6 knots boat speed and sailing at an angle of 98 degrees. The hydro-generator is pumping out 24 amps and I am consuming 15 amps with full lights blazing on deck before going to sleep for two hours.

Why am I away doing this lap of the planet? With political uncertainty, Brexit, economic problems, housing crisis and hospital trolleys, why run such an event? Some say it's madness (and I'm inclined to agree) but that's just a convenient way to describe what we can't describe or something we do not, or cannot, understand — such as the concept of infinity.

That question about the race was best articulated by a French socialist politician representing the Vendée region. He was rationalising why his local government office was sponsoring the event.

"It's a celebration of the environment, the elements, life itself and man taking on the odds," he said as he proceeded to dig into his wine and cheese at the cocktail reception.

In Ireland he might be seen as a 'smoked salmon socialist'.

But we must move the cheese, cast a line, catch the salmon and dream, challenge ourselves, set targets — whatever they may be — and go for it. Is to dream to do? Is a bad thought actually bad or a crime? Is to think to do?

It is by paraphrasing Thomas Moore, that today's Log ends:

'I've often been told by learned shipmates
That wishing and the crime are one,
And Heaven punishes desires
As much as if the deed were done.
'If wishing damns us, you and I
Are damned to all our heart's content

Come, then, at least we may enjoy
Some pleasures for our punishment
on the ocean wave.'

And to conclude, this night at sea, sure some day we'll be a long- time dead. So do it, whatever it may be.

Δ Day 19/20

Going into darkness of Day 20 we are moving quickly at 11 knots-plus in 9.5 knots of breeze at an angle of 110 degrees. It has been a frustrating two days. In desperation I took to reading some poetry, having a go at the whistle and going to the movies.

As time passes you become much more at one with the boat, nature, the elements and even time. Governed not so much by a clock other than when the sun rises and sets, the rhythm of the day and the needs of the boat, I am oblivious to external forces.

Whether gybing, reefing, changing sail, navigating, cooking, just plain goofing off reading (isn't Kindle brilliant?) or watching a movie (our on-board theatre has 150) daily existence enters another dimension.

My humour varies massively through the day. I enjoy my little victories such as finally getting the port hydro-generator back working. With little wind and slow speed, tensions can run high. Things become more relaxed as the wind pressure builds and we get moving. Until, of course, it becomes scary with too much wind. Never happy.

An important part of regulating life on the ocean is the daily meeting of the South Atlantic Residents Association. They are an erratic, unpredictable bunch. Some have big egos, others can be humble, others brave. They have big personalities to manage and meetings can be contentious. Did I mention the stupid ones? Here on board the Kilcullen Voyager, I have to handle all those personality types.

One member, for example, in the pitch black of night with no moon, wanted to go on the foredeck and change sail from the blast Reacher to the A3 Asymmetrical spinnaker. The more conservative element won out and we waited until dawn.

The entire weather situation, as well as deciding which route to take, is a complex issue. The ideal scenario is to move along the permanent cold front or SACZ. It reaches out across the south Atlantic from Brazil. Low pressures run along it and tend to form close to Itajai. The ideal scenario is to move along between one of these lows and the St Helena south Atlantic High. Over the next week it will be interesting to see how the scenarios pan out.

Meanwhile, assuming we get through this 20th night at sea, we look forward to breakfast and porridge with some of the Revive Active supplements from Galway mixed in.

Δ Day 21

No time for lunch

It was like a sudden wake-up call when the anticipated wind shift came. From 9 knots of warm north-westerly to a chilling south easterly at 20 knots. The sea was angry. That is how Day 21 started.

No more South Atlantic Residents Association debates.

Now was a call to arms. The banging and rattling of the carbon boat was like being tumbled around in a washing machine. While they are capable, these IMOCA 60s are not designed to go upwind.

These past 48 hours we've been on a deep dive straight south. After negotiating the permanent cold front coming across from Brazil or the SAZC, we have now headed west of the bunch. The hope is to get down the ice zone and Roaring Forties pronto. It's a calculated risk.

Another 'wake up' was an unexpected landfall in the

middle of the ocean. We almost ran into the Brazilian Atlantic islands, Ilas Martin Vaz, 600 miles off the coast. I passed within two miles of Ilha da Trindade, the largest at 620 metres high and 10 sq km in area. It was majestic rising out of the skyline.

I never knew they existed. They are only visible when you enlarge the electronic charts. They look spectacular and represent another little-known destination to put on the bucket list when I have more time.

That's the bizarre thing about a race around the world; there are so many wonderful places to stop for lunch — only there is no time.

The boat is working 24/7, or 24/8. You must be constantly on the alert for wear and tear. When it all works it's brilliant. When it goes wrong it's usually big because of the scale and the loads involved.

This morning on a routine 'residents association stroll' on foredeck, I saw the Blast Reacher roller furling line as if it was almost about to break from chafe.

If so, the entire sail could unfurl in a blow, damage the sail and be a nightmare to get down. It took 20 minutes of intense physical work to sort it out.

During the afternoon, I opened the engine cover to discover the base almost flooded. The engine and electric pump did not work so it took me 40 minutes to get all the water out manually.

Left unchecked for a few more days we could have lost the engine and a valuable source of charging our battery as it complements the two hydro-generators. I think the water is draining in from the water ballast tanks. That's another issue to be solved tomorrow.

Moving south each day you can feel the temperature drop. You can see the crisp sharp cold almost on the ocean, rolling over the swell that is building. Often a sign of impending heavy weather, it is also a forerunner of the Roaring Forties where the sea rolls around the bottom of the world without interruption and icebergs.

△ Day 23

Again, what a difference a day makes. Early morning, after two days on the wind, it's getting colder. So I finally, with reluctance, got into my thermals. Like the good boy scout's motto: I was prepared.

Yet by midday I was naked to the waist, making the 380 turns of the winch grinder — the amount necessary to shake the reef out of the mainsail.

The wind moved more to the north, below 10 knots for a time and we had a marvellous day sailing. It was one of those times when it was good to be alive. We are reaching south and east. We are getting closer to the Antarctic and the cold — like turkeys voting for Christmas.

What is also interesting is that the group of 10 teams east and north are moving slowly and having difficulty getting south. All going well a low pressure system will shortly come in from the west and we will ride the top of it in 25 knot+ winds.

Cape of Good Hope here we come.

And I am catching the fleet.

One wonders where time goes. Between the 'office' and constant boat work, the days just disappear. I am overworked but happy. So much so that my SARA (South Atlantic Residents Association) union shop steward lodged a complaint over my 25:8 work schedules instead of the normal 24:7.

Via a live TV link to Paris, I was reconnected with race commentator Sir Robin Knox-Johnston, who gave me good advice. His is one of many chat shows built around the race. Indeed people watching and tracking each boat often know more about what's going on than the unfortunate skippers. So it was interesting to listen to the commentators.

I last sailed with Robin in a successful Round Ireland run on his then catamaran British Airways. The trip hit world headlines because, to our surprise, Jenny Guinness joined us. Because she had been kidnapped (though she had the name, her family did not have the Guinness wealth and the kidnappers had made a big mistake) we assumed she would pull out. But just a few days after being released she joined us on the record trip.

The cabin of Kilcullen was about the same size as the space in which Jenny had to live with her captor until she was found.

A born survivor, she made friends and built relationships with the small-time criminals so they would not kill, or hurt, her.

Some months later one of the kidnapper's wives delivered a daughter who was promptly named Jennifer. Only in Ireland.

On the subject of babies my 'big' sister Pauline's daughter, Nicola, recently gave birth to baby Jamie. Congratulations! Our families keep expanding. Let's celebrate how great the Irish are at making babies. Any idea why?

Pauline was complimentary about this (near-daily) voyage log. I thank her and am pleasantly surprised someone is reading this guff from a demented sailor boy.

It's 10 minutes short of midnight. Time to conclude, trim the sails and take a nap. And then we'll launch into November 29th.

It is an important day for my daughter Saoirse. It's her birthday. While meaning 'freedom' in English, Saoirse was the first Irish boat to circumnavigate the world with the country's new flag back in the 1920s. It was skippered by Limerick man Conor O'Brien. Happy birthday Saoirse.

◢ Day 24

Moving south east, we are not getting the 25 knots hoped for to slip us fast below the pack.

However, I did trim my beard.

We have had a steady 6 to 19 knots this past 24 hours. Being almost downwind, it is not good. We need an angle of at least 135 degrees to keep optimum speed.

This has pulled us more north — where the pressure is less — than planned. The big tactical decision now is when, or if, to gybe back down for a short-term loss and possible long-term gain. Ideally it should be done on a wind shift.

Again, it has been a really busy day on board. Time flies and the mind wanders. Inanimate objects start to take on their own personality. Take rope as an example. This boat is full of it. Different strengths, uses, materials and pliability. With 62 different control lines, all coming back into the cockpit, they need to be constantly coiled, sorted and managed so that the chaos can be organised when the manure hits the fan.

Each rope takes on a personality. All are card-carrying members of the Residents Association (SARA). Some are a pleasure to coil, work with and handle; others are difficult, kink and always seem to get in a knot.

A reflection of life and people?

The green furling line for the enormous A3 downwind sail comes to mind. It always seems to get in a mess and the furling gives endless trouble.

By contrast the reef clew lines on the main always work well, as do the cute little 'Lazy Jacks' lines that keep the runner secure.

I talk to the ropes; sometimes in jest and often in anger. Some even answer back.

Moving from plant to animal life, each machine on the

JOURNEY TO THE EDGE

boat starts to take on a living personality.

The self-steering system is called Molly Malone. Molly seldom complains, hardly ever stops — except in extreme conditions — and most days simply gets on with it. I talk to her all the time. She is great company and really reliable.

The two hydro-generators, or the 'terrible twins' as I call them, are contrary. While they look identical, one churns out twice the electricity charge of the other. The same personalisation continues with all the equipment on the boat.

The one piece of equipment (for want of a better word) the boat lacks is a mirror. If there is one, I can't see it. Men seldom spend time contemplating their reflection. Perhaps the symbol of manliness should be an inverse relationship to the time spent looking at oneself in the mirror?

Anyway, today when it came to trimming my beard — for a video log to send to my sponsors BIOLINE for their conference, the mirror was a real problem.

My lady commandant prefers short beards, as do I — a Number 2 to be precise. For these reasons today's video log shows me trimming the beard. The camera became a substitute for a mirror, and while at it why not log it? I was able to trim using the screen as my mirror.

Therefore: camera, camera on the wall who is the prettiest of them all? Reply: most definitely not the skipper of the Kilcullen Voyager.

I am happy out, with it newly trimmed.

And on behalf of SARA: Sláinte and thanks again for your interest from the southern Ocean.

Δ Day 25/26

Tristan da Cunha majestically rose out of the mist, 6,600

feet tall and seven miles long. We passed within two miles and talked via VHF with Radio Tristan. Our passing was big news in a place where little happens.

Hardly anyone visits; there are 264 residents who collectively own the island. It is said to be the world's most remote inhabited archipelago. And, if there is a prize in the race for the skipper who has gone closest to the many Atlantic Islands, I stake my claim (starting with the Canaries).

Around 1,235 miles from its closest neighbour St Helena, it is accessible only by a six-day boat journey from South Africa or as part of an epic month-long cruise through the South Atlantic Ocean.

Tristan is about as far from a quick holiday destination as it gets.

You would have to think long and hard for it to be on your 'bucket-list'.

It was originally annexed by the British in 1816 because they feared the French would use it as a base to rescue the exiled Napoleon on St Helena. But despite its formidable remoteness, Tristan da Cunha, named after the eponymous Portuguese explorer, has a rich history and plethora of unique native wildlife.

The second last big event there was in 1961 when Queen Mary's Peak erupted and all had to be evacuated. Fortunately there was little damage and the residents returned to the Edinburgh of the Seven Seas, the main settlement.

The lobster factory is the biggest income earner for residents — all of whom are listed as farmers. They also share in the work of the community which includes several government jobs.

The last big event? It was when Kenny Read and his Puma team spent several weeks there after losing their mast in the Volvo Ocean Around the World race. Apparently, the islanders adopted the crew and the few single local girls did not want them to leave.

Before Tristan, which we passed with 30 knots plus of wind, two reefs in the main and no headsail, the new reality on board Kilcullen kicked in the morning of Day 25.

Winds were at 35 knots-plus. One surf down a wave brought us above 26 knots — that's 40km an hour. I also foolishly got soaked wet when engulfed by a wave while struggling on deck.

It took almost two hours to shorten sail and I had to hunker down on all fours and crawl forward to the bow to solve a roller-furling problem.

One moment we would rise, ride a wave. You'd feel on top of the world. Then there would be a massive surge where you'd be planted between two walls of water.

We have dug south to get wind and by the 'Hook' we have it. It is an extraordinary contrast from idyllic light air sailing in the tropics 10 days ago.

Hook, from Hook Head off Waterford, is a term dating back to Cromwell. It is where I made landfall after crossing the Atlantic in my 16-foot dinghy. We'll get there "by Hook or by Crook" Cromwell reputedly said. Crook is a West Cork headland.

Cromwell would have been sailing from the south coast of England and planning to land somewhere between the two.

Anyway, we had had the Blast Reacher and one reef in the main when the wind came. First it was down to the J2 and another reef in the main. Now it's main only and we still get 20 knots. Since problems off the Canaries with the second reef, this was the first time to test my new system. The first time the load was too great and the line broke. The second time with a different configuration we got the reef in and, here in the southern ocean, it may be some time before we have to get it out.

Meanwhile following the Tristan da Cunha triumph there was a special EGM of the South Atlantic Residents Association.

I am honoured to have been elected as President. The inauguration will be the same day as President Trump takes his oath of office in Washington.

Alan Roura, on board La Barbeque representing Switzerland in the Vendée, will be the First Minister and Deputy First Minister combined.

I am especially saddened to learn of the withdrawal of Kojiro Shiraishi from the race. It's a big upset from a personal perspective. We were first introduced in an Irish pub in Tokyo eight years ago and built a friendship.

He brought his samurai sword and I brought my Irish whistle. I have never seen a blade as sharp. I was also impressed by the sharpness of his personality. I am not so sure about the whistle.

We had kept in contact; our friendship deepened through the build-up to the Vendée. Also the Japanese team has a special Irish interest in that it is superbly managed by Tony O'Connor of Raheny, Dublin.

Tony's wife is Japanese. His language and business skills made the project possible — and the team qualified.

Not being a French or European team, it was an added achievement to get to the start line for Kojiro. Such is the nature of this weird and wonderful event, encompassing every aspect of humanity, that we never know what's going to happen next. Skippers live on the edge 24 hours a day.

At least there is some consolation for Kojiro in that it is summer in Cape Town and they have good golf. He is passionate about the sport; we had a great game just prior to the start.

Δ Day 30

It has been a full day. It stretched from an early-morning encounter with another competitor, talking by Skype with enthusiastic school children, to some personality clashes on the governing board of Residents Association.

Our imminent entry to the Indian Ocean has added to tensions on board.

It was just after first light that I came within one mile of Alan Roura, on La Fabrique. His sponsors range from the Interactive restaurant store complex of the same name to the city and canton of Geneva, 7 Seas, Ropeye and several more Swiss firms. It was my first sighting of another entry for four weeks.

Alan was fast asleep while his boat sailed happily along. She looked well as I sailed past. He and she faded through the brightening air. There was no response to my VHF or telephone calls and my email. I became a little concerned. We had been in regular contact and a comfort for each other since we had gone away south on our own from the main bunch.

To date this seems to have worked well since we have both made reasonable gains. Yet both of us say we are not so concerned about the racing and just want to get around the planet. Like hell.

He's a great sailor with a strong personality; we have connected well. Previously when he took a 50-mile detour along the north-west coast of Brazil within three miles of the coast, I was concerned for him.

It transpired he did it to get within GSM range and to download software to solve some problems. It was with the approval of the race committee, since mobile phones are not allowed.

I need not have been concerned today. On awakening Alan called on the VHF and we had a great chat. All was well. He had just been really tired after a difficult four or five days through the gale we shared. Such remote camaraderie runs deep. "Nobody can really understand what it's like," Alan explained. In truth, most are smart enough not to find out.

Another highlight today was a Skype connection to St Conleth's College in Dublin. Teachers Gavin Maguire and Tony Kilcommons were enthusiastic. It was organised by Noel Rabbitte of MSL Mercedes-Benz Ballsbridge Motors, sponsors of our schools' programme. We have had great take-up at primary school level and the bigger Atlantic Youth Trust charity's mission to connect youth with ocean and adventure.

The questions and interest from the classroom were excellent, uplifting. On Skype I was able to explain different aspects of the boat. We had four cameras — including one on the mast looking forward — connected to the big screen in the classroom.

I even went for a walk on the foredeck with the camera on and one child was worried I might fall over. He was glad when he saw me get back to the safety of the cockpit — 8,000 miles away on the southern ocean.

Meanwhile we are due to talk live with Ryan Tubridy on Wednesday morning on progress to date.

We've also had an emergency council meeting of the Residents Association. Apparently Mr Marlboro on the foredeck got soaking wet when Molly Malone, self-steering department, altered course upwind instead of downwind. I also feel there is a little insecurity and concern over our move to the Indian Ocean.

I thank Richard Moore for his comments on how I celebrated the start of my 5th week with a change of underwear. He says:

"Make sure you don't exhaust your fresh underwear sup-

ply. You could quadruple your range by remembering to wear as follows:
- *Forwards*
- *Backwards*
- *Inside-out forwards*
- *Inside-out backwards."*

Great advice; and let's keep it just that.

LESSONS FROM CHAPTER 9

↗ Often it is a case that to finish is to win.

↗ Be prepared... Being caught off guard is what gets you.

Chapter 10
Indian Ocean

W E passed well south of the Cape of Good Hope which, one time long ago was better named as the Cape of Storms. Where the Atlantic and the Indian Ocean meet is a wild spot. We were moving fast and progress was good. Soon we were edging slowly down deeper into strong winds as each few days we moved a little up the fleet. At this stage we were 15th out of the 29 starters, which was great.

Δ Day 32

They call this the Roaring Forties for a good reason. It roars. We had a rebate of 12 hours, sunshine and winds of only 20 knots. This allowed repairs, sort-out and a key meeting of the Association. Then it swiftly powered back again to 30 knot-plus. It's relentless.

Our worry is that since the wind had moved into the north, we could run out of sea room to avoid the ice exclusion zone. This is a line, currently running parallel to our course about 50 miles south — and fewer than three hours at current speeds.

The wind chill and cold are severe. We have made the remarkable discovery that when you run out of dry socks it's good to plant your feet in the sleeves of a jumper or a jacket. Of course that's only for the cabin. It's not practical on deck: you just hop into your boots and moist socks regardless.

On deck I am also concerned about not being seen, or running into something, as we have lost our radar dome with the Active Echo attached.

This is a clever device. It gives an alert of other ships from the scan of the radar. They will always have their radars on but may not see you or regard a small boat as just 'clutter' on the screen.

This issue, among other serious survival matters, was discussed at length by the Residents Association. After heated debate, which helped warm the cabin, by majority decision it was decided to merge SARA with the IORA under a new name. Therefore the South Atlantic Residents Association Indian Ocean Residents Association will be part of the greater and more powerful SORA — South Atlantic Residents Association.

I was personally flattered, in my ultimate moments of magnificent modesty, to be elected president of the new entity.

The sailing and sea, day after day, are relentless and seem eternal. The sea is so powerfully in harmony with the wind. When angry, nothing is sacred or left intact. When calm, she can be the most magic, colourful and happy place to be in tune with nature and the environment.

We had some escape from ocean fury last night at the SORA inaugural dinner dance.

I thank Michael Morpurgo from 'Alone on a Wide Wide Sea' via Captain John McDonald (a friend who supported the campaign) for the following words:

'That's what sailing is, a dance. And your partner is the sea. And with the sea you never take liberties. You ask her, you don't tell her. You have to remember always that she's the leader, not you. You and your boat are dancing to her tune'.

Δ Day 33

The questions, feedback and fascination of the children from our schools' programme following the race are fantastic. While designed for primary schools in the 8-12-year category, I copy this email from Kevin Cronin in Bunclody.

"Hi Enda,

The first and second years of Bunclody Vocational College have followed you closely since 13:02 on 6/11/16. We are cheering you on and wishing you all the best. Your race is full of the most exciting Maths, Technology, Science and Geography.

"Not to mention heroism and human endeavour. We have dedicated a full notice board to your race and pin up daily progress reports and chart updates. You are also our main focus for Science Week (this week). Hope we can stay in touch and that it's not a problem us not being a primary school."

Thanks Kevin. Unfortunately, it is hard for me to respond to all. The most I can do is sail merrily along and do the best I can from the carnage to finish the race. Other than the Log and the odd video it's impossible for me to engage with the questions.

Here we thank Neil O'Hagan for driving this aspect of the voyage; he knows more than I anyway, and can come to me with the tricky questions.

Such as the one from a child who asked why I told fibs about my Atlantic crossing in the inflatable. He said his dad said I made it up. Now that's clever. Perhaps I did? However, it's hard to deny the photographic evidence. Hopefully the child will not grow up to be as cynical as his dad, though a dose of healthy scepticism is no harm at all.

Finally, for all gathered at Howth today for the Christmas charity lunch, with Marcus Hutchinson our project director as guest speaker, I wish you well.

Also, Kieran Jameson (sail maker for our Mini-Transat Race many years ago) should be thanked for emptying three bottles at Cape Hope, Leewin and Horn.

We're on mission.

Δ Day 35

This is hard.

So that I can never, ever do something like this again, I will sign a legal binding document and give it to somebody in trust allowing them to stop me from ever, ever, ever doing something like this again.

It is tough.

It is cold.

It is wet.

And to think I did it of my own free will — to live on the edge with constant challenges. The mind boggles; 'tis bonkers.

That said, I am thrilled to have survived thus far. It has been an extraordinary adventure and personal journey — psychologically and physically. And a good way to get fit.

I am lucky and honoured to fly the flag and be in a position to have a go. The race organisers do a brilliant job. Thanks Laura, Jacques and team. It is just wonderful to be part of it. It is great to feel the emotional support, the passion, the ocean — man against the elements and all that.

From reports, some other skippers seem to have had it tougher. I feel for them, and note Conrad Coleman has been performing extraordinary feats. Taking a line from Mich Desj', two-time winner of the Vendée Globe: you need to be mentally prepared for one major problem each day.

On board Kilcullen a mirror would have been useful. A sheet was jammed around the rudder and I could not see how or why. It was dangerous on the rudder and would not come clear. It would have been handy to have had a mirror to 'look around' the edge to see the problem.

In the end, we did an Alex Thomson. We canted the keel the wrong way and hardened the sails for the boat to heel and go more upwind. This worked. She was remarkably steady going along at an angle of about 60 degrees.

Then I climbed out over the stern and stood on the aft ledge and the port rudder was clear out of the water so that I was able to stand on it. Later that day a starboard sheet caught itself around the hydro-generator. Not as extreme, but another problem to be solved.

And having set out just to get around, it's grand to be 15th. And it's been brilliant racing, working to stay ahead of the American Rick Wilson, Alan Roura from Switzerland and Eric Bellion of France.

When the wind goes lighter we close up — and I suffer not being able to fly my asymmetrical sails. At some stages, we have been extremely close; we chat by email. At one time, I had warm VHF conversations with Alan; the mutual respect and support for what each is going through was powerful.

Our next landmark is the Kerguelen Islands, about 600 miles east. I am contemplating whether or not to pull in there to sort out my halyard problems and climb the mast.

After that it's Cape Leeuwin off Australia the second of the Big Three. And after that it's Cape Horn.

It's like eating the proverbial elephant, each day, a little bit at a time.

Δ Day 37

Rather than stop in the lee of the Kerguelen Islands to sort out our mast halyard problem, the Residents Association elected to do it on the green, open ocean. It was completed at heavy personal cost; I had to climb a mast in 20 knots of wind and a big rolling sea without solving the problem. It was like driving a car with one gear.

With a big storm ahead, we needed to be able to set our smallest J4 sail and the J3. This was the lesser evil based on advice from Commander Marcus.

To say it was a nightmare would be an understatement. It was physically exhausting and a massive psychological effort to pull myself up a mast while rolling around in the ocean.

I'd done a short practice climb before the start of the race but the real thing was totally different. I was terrified. But it had to be done. As they say, there is "nothing like a hanging" to focus the mind.

It took several hours to recover from the slow, cautious climb, using special mountaineering equipment. I thought I knew how it worked but found I did not. Thanks to a guidance illustration from Commander Marcus, at base, the matter was solved.

What had been a simple problem, the breaking of Lazy Jacks holding up the boom, became a complex problem. It was the use of the J4 Halyard to hold the boom up and when this line broke, the halyard went out of control wrapping itself around all the others and the broken Lazy Jacks. It even extended to wrapping around the head of the furled J3- thereby making it unusable.

But properly under way we got back on track and passed the Kerguelen Islands in the black of night. They are named after the French explorer of the same name. Even to go there then (1772) was an incredible achievement, given the ships they had and types of underwear to keep them warm.

Around 2,570 square metres in total — or about 60 x 70 miles — they are regarded as one of the most isolated places on earth.

They have no residents as such, just some scientists carrying out research. Historically it was a base for whaling and sealing, but no more. By all accounts the climate is horrible, although they are a district of France.

Meanwhile the weather forecast is not good. There is a massive low coming through. Some boats have opted to go north and over the top. We are now committed to going along the bottom close to the ice exclusion zone. It will be a rough ride but we're up for it.

The plan is to reach Cape Leeuwin and South Australia within a week, in time for Christmas. Remember though, the closest we are likely to get to Australia is 400 miles as we head for New Zealand and Cape Horn.

Δ Day 38

Going to bed in your long johns, top layers, huddled in one sleeping bag, inside another sleeping bag with a sleeping cap to boot — and one eye almost always on the compass and wind instruments — would swiftly shatter your romantic notions.

I'm sure, as light is day, if this is their summer I would rather have two mothers-in-law (the Irish penalty for bigamy) than spend winter here. Being absent and abstinent do make the heart grow fonder. A bit like how the madman replied when asked why he was banging his head against the bed post: "Sure it's great when you stop."

And that's how I sleep in the cold southern ocean from time to time. I'm always on an extra alert position to changes in movement by the boat. Like a musician playing an instrument, the sailor instinctively knows if there is something not quite right. Lovers are the same.

Day 38 was similar: a steady 20 to 22 knots. We're 120 degrees and due east in an overcast sky with trouble brewing; 40-knot winds are expected soon.

Our risk here is that the wind would move more north and east meaning we'd have little sea room to run before it and avoid the Ice Line.

Of course, the advantage of what we are doing is that we would sail a shorter distance and gain ground on some boats on their northern route, taking the top end of the depression. Determined as we are not to mind the race — just to finish — it is tough to suppress those competitive juices.

As a contrast to storm watching, now that your SORA president (elect) is totally removed from the so called 'land-of-the-living' for almost 40 days, we did a live TV interview, direct to race headquarters, alongside the Eiffel Tower in Paris.

Her Excellency, Geraldine Byrne Nason, our highly-regarded Irish Ambassador to France, was in the studio for the interview. Kindly facilitated by Commander Marcus, we talked directly and managed a 'piosa beag as Gaeilge' as we spoke about Ireland's relationship with France, the maritime, the passion and so on.

Sadly, I learned of the death of the poet John Montague.

It is appropriate that we should finish our live Indian Ocean link with the final stanza of his poem 'Wild Water'.

Born in County Tyrone in 1929, JM was essentially Ireland's poet laureate. He lived his final years in Paris and was buried in Dublin this week.

'luminous, bleached -
white water –
that light in the narrows
before a storm breaks'

Δ Days 41, 42 & 43

With two nasty blows in quick succession we had a tiring few days. They included a bad knock when our computer navigation system crashed. That means it's back to the

Off Port-la-Forêt, Brittany, December 20, 2015. Crossing the finishing line; 3rd in the Solo Atlantic Race from St. Barts, thus qualifying to start the Vendée in November 2016.

Headsail torn to shreds off the Azores following 50-knot winds when it was too dangerous to go on deck to fix the damaged roller furling.

After finishing the Atlantic Race, lifting the port hydrogenerator which produced up to 40 amps — making the Kilcullen self-sufficient for energy.

Celebrating after crossing the line.

The boat shuddered with a massive bang off the Cliffs of Moher. The rudder was split in half and I suspect it mortally wounded a basking shark.

At the helm, early morning off the coast of Brittany on the way to Le Sables d'Olonne for the start.

"I have spread my dreams under your feet. Tread softly because you tread on my dreams."
W.B. Yeats.

Enda O'Coineen

On the foredeck powering downwind.

Friends and family on the pontoon soaking up the electric atmosphere prior to the start. Left to right: Sean Lemass, Louis Ronaldson, Nicola, Aoife Nolan. David Beattie and my sisters Annmarie Bowring and Pauline Moran.

Preparing freeze-dried food supplies for four months at sea, in bags, each numbered, to be opened one day at a time and adjusted for likely climatic conditions.

Local Irish and French supporters the night before at 'Le Galway' pub, led by Sheena Kelleher (right), from Ballinasloe and her wonderful family, who are living in Les Sables d'Olonne.

My good friends Micheal and Cormac O'hAmhlain who travelled from the Aran Islands to play and make the party for the send-off with the Unthinkable Bodhrán Player making up "The Unsinkable Kilcullen Music Team". It was a mighty celebration excuse. Many other friends and supporters alongside ranged from Cabinet Minister Simon Coveney, to Philippe Mangan, President INVIVO, the largest French farming group.

Heading away into the Atlantic and the Mercedes logo from MSL Motors who were very generous, thanks to Stephen O'Flaherty, in supporting our Atlantic Youth Trust Schools Programme to follow the adventure.

The hands of friendship, the heart and the relationship crowned...the iconic Claddagh Ring – one of the few symbols representing Ireland which are not shamrocks, harps or Celtic cross religious icons.

With over 80 control lines coming into the cockpit, it can get very messy after rapid sail manoeuvres (or a bad storm) and needs constant rope coiling and tidying...

Moving south to warmer waters was magic and brought its own gifts. Here I am with one of the first flying fish to land on deck. The first one hit the boat like the sound of a bullet in darkness and gave me a fright.

My old Dubarry boots from Ballinasloe are robust, waterproof and a must-have to provide that comfort factor for any serious ocean sailor.

Moving deep into the South Atlantic, leaving Tristan da Cunha to port and covered in cloud. With a population of about 250, it's one of many extraordinary and remote inhabited islands in the world.

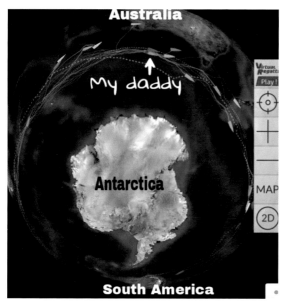

Viewing our planet from the bottom shows the race fleet literally sailing around Antarctica — the shortest distance between Australia and Cape Horn is literally through the South Pole.

Right: President Higgins kindly tried to call on Christmas Day but failed to connect on the satellite phone. Many thoughtful friends and family had packed presents which were wonderful to indulge.

One of many views from astern of the vast ocean with its many humours, sea conditions and lighting.

Christmas Day with Alan Roura of Switzerland and Eric Bellion of France some hundreds of miles south of Tasmania. It suited us to suspend racing and we were deliberately slowing up to stay behind a massive depression ahead, off New Zealand.

In an instant, my world fell apart and the entire rig was in the ocean.

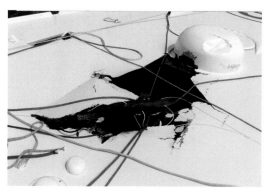

As the mast erupted, it left a gaping hole, and the seas washed in, 180 miles from the nearest land and beyond the reach of the rescue services.

Using the full length carbon battens I was able to mount them like a 'wigwam tent' and hoist a headsail to eventually get underway very slowly, taking a week to make the nearest land. I was determined not to be rescued.

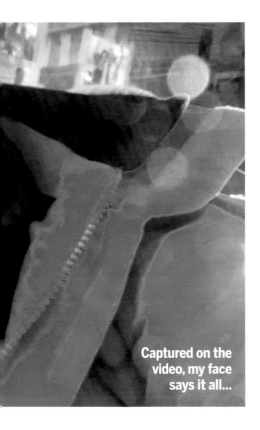

Captured on the video, my face says it all...

Captured by the *Otago Times*, a day after berthing in Dunedin, Otago Bay where I was competing on the front page with the local penguin population. Steve Little, a fisherman, kindly towed me in for the last few miles. He accommodated me above his pub, The Carey's Bay Inn in Port Chalmers — where Ernest Shackleton had sailed from 100 years previously to the month.

Through our Atlantic Youth Trust link with the New Zealand Spirit of Adventure Trust, I was welcomed with open arms into the family of Tony Cummins or "BBQ Bill" who were fantastic in helping me on my way. "We are very religious," says Tony. "And we would go to Church on a Sunday to pray for crop failure," while he went on to explain that was because on Saturday night, "we would sow our wild oats!"

A week later, a large group of well-wishers — including Irish musicians — came down for our send-off from Dunedin with a temporary rig.

Under way again headed north with a temporary rig towards Christchurch. We had some challenges, putting bits of the boat and her skipper back together, as we navigated up along the New Zealand coast.

At the helm, Paddy O'Connor, a former member of the Irish Naval Service and team member from our NCB Whitbread Around the World Team, came to help me in difficulties and we had some fun.

time of the steam engine in some respects. We are using paper charts. However, this log was recorded over the sat phone.

Quite often after a bad patch you feel: "That's it. Finished." But for resilience to recover and mend things I decided to get away from the ice exclusion zone, even though it's the shortest and windiest route, to get a couple of hundred miles towards Perth. "Wouldn't that be a great place for Christmas in the height of their summer?"

Now two days later, following a hike south, we're back in the race again. We're powering along at 15 knots in 22 knots of wind although sailing a little blind. The sun has returned. It has warmed up. I've gone from three layers to two.

Things are looking up but the first blow was hard going. I was miserable. It was overcast, cold and wet and I was living constantly on the edge, wondering would the next fall and wave be the one?

Then we had respite for 10 hours before it raged again. The wind speed read 50 knots at times.

I was in my sleeping bag when I heard a roar. The side became the roof as I scrambled to find my Dubarry boots. Whatever else, even stark naked, without good boots to climb and crawl to take action I'm helpless. After a clatter below I climbed out topside.

It was strangely tranquil.

That was because the boat was on her side. Effectively there was no mast or sails to catch the wind. The cantilevered keel made it worse, with the main backed and jammed against what was the weather runner.

So first I triggered the keel and slowly released the runner. I made sure to pull back on the lazy jacks, otherwise it would catch in the main. Eventually we got moving again and set about sorting out the mess.

I don't mind telling you it shook me.

Later on deck as I stood between the mast and daggerboard sorting out a sheet, the nose of the boat dived into a wave. A wall of water dragged and slapped me into the daggerboard. That effectively saved me from going over but my leg did slip, straining my pelvis. I was lucky the damage was not greater than strained ligaments.

My work ranges from fixing the hydro generator, splicing some line, fixing the starboard main winch and so on but we still do not have the computer up and running. Backups are a problem. Hopefully it will be ready for Christmas. If not we can continue even if somewhat handicapped.

Helpfully, the race committee has given me formal permission to get weather information by phone.

Meanwhile the race trundles on. My only contacts are by phone and touching base with my regular Southern Ocean Residents Association colleagues at meetings where different parts of my mind argue, play games and entertain itself.

Δ Days 44 & 45

Our capacity to adjust to new realities is amazing: like losing an arm or leg or, in my case, a computer navigation system. You realise that you can do without something you thought you could not.

But right now, I'm nervous and afraid.

We are going along the bottom of Australia and preparing for the vast unknown of the South Pacific before it meets the Antarctic. It's disturbing to hear that, in recent days, we have lost two, possibly three more boats. One was due to a collision, another lost a mast, and most recently our friend, Paul Meilhart of SMA, had a keel hydraulic problem.

At least there is my surprise Christmas package to look forward to on Day 50 at sea. It should be somewhere south of Tasmania — though I confess to digging into the chocolates last week during one of the storms.

After our backup system failed to work I was disorientated. I said I could not continue, particularly with no internet connection to the outside world, no weather information, no news on other boats and so on.

Now a few days later I have readjusted to the new reality and I'm back in our 'chart' around the planet. The outside world will also be spared pictures and videos of the SORA president elect and the antics on board the Kilcullen.

There was also a quiet satisfaction in passing Rick Wilson the other night on his Great American IV boat. A deep-thinking, brilliant man, he has a degree in mathematics from Harvard and MIT and an impressive schools programme; 300,000 children follow his adventure.

But rather than looking at what is not working, I look at what I have. There is a satellite phone, the boat is functioning, we have a GPS position and paper charts. We're not that badly off.

We're also constantly looking to find solutions and make do with what we've got. On the positive side too, the rest of our ship is in good shape. The main exception is the reefing problems on the main (which is important in storms). My daily routine and maintenance programme never ends.

And I learned of a message from a young follower, Milos in Paris, today. I'll have to wait until my computer is back up and running to see the card but thank you. It's somewhat strange to think you're all at home following this adventure. I can assure you it means a lot to me. The complexity of getting these logs to you is now greatly increased but I will endeavour to keep it up.

Δ Days 46 & 47

We're in deep fog; visibility is down to a few yards. The wind has dropped back to 15 knots. It's wet with a constant drizzle — yet I spent several happy hours on deck. It was the first time the wind was under 20 knots in almost three weeks and got back to a sort of normality as we now power along some 400 miles south west of Tasmania.

I can report that I am also fighting a psychological mid-voyage crisis. The sheer isolation, not knowing what will happen next, keeps my brain in orbit. It is not helped by being on the backup autopilot, having no computer and comms. Without proper information it's hard to compete but I'm lucky to be close to the other boats.

The entire engineering department of the Southern Ocean Residents Association is working to solve the various problems on board.

I'm also acutely aware the supplies need to be monitored. What seemed like an abundance before is now reassessed and measured — from paper towels to gas for the stove — so we'll have enough to complete the voyage. Having enough diesel to keep the battery charging is a concern too as this is a means of complementing the hydro generators (one of which is not working).

On deck the big issue is not being able to reef the mainsail in heavy air.

And to think we're not even half way.

At times, I despair. Other times I just exist.

But today, after many hours of hard physical work we've actually had a good result.

Setting the A3 spinnaker up alone is a major task. It starts with lifting the massive sail out of the forepeak; all 280 square metres of it out through the small forehatch.

Setting up the sheets, and eventually the hoist, is really

hard work. Normally it's a task for five or six people on a boat this size.

It's surreal here as I move along in the fog, totally alone, deep in the southern ocean. Yet the fact we are sailing as a group is a strong comfort should something go wrong in this remote location.

A final thought: wouldn't it be fun if all of us in the group downed sails and got together on Christmas Day? It would be a bit like the battlefront in the First World War.

Happy Christmas to all.

LESSONS FROM CHAPTER 10
- ↗ You realise you can do without some things that you thought you could not.
- ↗ Rather than looking at what is not working, I look at what I have.

Some 400 miles south of Tasmania, we exchanged gifts and, in my case, sang some Christmas carols. I also gave Alan a memory-stick with more than 100 movies — and a cigar. He was ecstatic.

Chapter 11
Christmas Day

WITH advice to slow down to avoid the worst of a storm, we thought we would make the most of the fact that three boats were in close proximity.

So with the other two skippers close by we decided to have our own Christmas party. After 50 days of racing 24/7, continually trying to get ahead of other boats, we called a truce, downed sails, slowed down, and rendezvoused in the middle of nowhere.

Some hundreds of miles south of Tasmania, we exchanged gifts and, in my case, sang some Christmas carols. I also gave Alan a memory-stick with more than 100 movies — and a cigar. He was ecstatic.

He bellowed back: "That will be the first cigar I've ever smoked." As the youngest in the race, he has to start sometime, though he'll be disappointed all the movies I gave him are respectable, not the pornographic ones I told him to expect.

Our most unusual meeting was akin to the scene in the trenches in the First World War. Imagine 100 years ago soldiers stopped shooting for a while in No Man's Land, met, shook hands, exchanged gifts and then went back into battle with each other.

Anyway I was dispatched a small bottle of whiskey and a lucky leprechaun by the others. Sadly, the throw was a foot short and, despite gallant efforts from Eric, it was lost to the ocean.

All three of us had no headsails, and reefed mainsails, and for 36 hours we were going slowly. That was to avoid sailing into a massive deep low pressure building south of New Zealand where the winds are set to reach 70 knots and the seas are up to 10 metres.

It has been a deeply emotional and moving day. Here on the ocean, I really appreciate the gifts from family and friends and the many Christmas greetings sent online. Brian Sheridan, Galway's harbourmaster, put a lot of thought into his package. Such support is invaluable for the next phase as we make for the Pacific Ocean and the much-anticipated rounding of Cape Horn. As we dive south again, we face a massive stretch of barren water ahead.

With the mast track now damaged at the first spreader it will be impossible to reef further or to take down the main. It looks like there will be some interesting heavy-weather sailing ahead. And we still are working away on resolving computer problems.

To top it all off we encountered a school of dolphins. Not the sort we're used to in Western Europe as they have a white stripe.

As I stood on the bow they ducked and dived while I talked to them. I wouldn't be surprised if they understood my incomprehensible mutterings. They were clearly conscious of life on deck.

¶ ¶ ¶ ¶

Following the buzz of Christmas and now 52 days at sea, I felt really alone. After the excitement of meeting up with two boats, we got moving with the worst of the storm gone ahead of us.

But I still had big problems on board. First it was the self-steering (my B&G equipment needed to be recalibrated) and second was the inability to either put a third reef in or shake out the first two.

Nonetheless progress was good crossing the Tasman Sea between Australia and New Zealand.

I started to explore options. What would be a good place to stop for repairs?

The two possibilities ahead were Campbell or Macquarie Islands. They are remote and rugged sub-Antarctic places. Campbell Island was once a huge sheep farm. But I gather it was too rough even for the sheep. And Macquarie Island was once a whaling station. Other than a few researchers it is now uninhabited. Oddly enough Macquarie is Australian territory although it's quite close to New Zealand.

In the end I made for the shelter of Stewart Island, south of South Island, New Zealand. That involved going north. It's a wild, rugged and beautiful place.

By email Marcus had sourced some more detailed charts and I managed to navigate into a small bay on the southern end. The plan was to anchor and repair the main track if possible and to recalibrate the instruments in flat water. It all seemed like a great idea at the time but it turned out to be a disaster.

First, my anchor would not hold. Even though the area was sheltered and the wind was light, the slightest puff made us drag anchor. It was getting dark. I decided to abort that mission and get out to sea where it was safer. Indeed, I came within a few feet of going aground and that would surely have been the end of the race for me.

Man, was I happy to get to sea again! I waited offshore overnight and came into the lee of the land the following day and successfully under-sailed and re-calibrated the compass and instruments. I did so thanks to John Malone who kindly volunteered his time to help. I think we were on the phone for more than three hours. The satellite phone bill came to more than €3,500 for that alone.

That evening I set sail for the Pacific Ocean, the International Date Line and Cape Horn. All was looking good as I sailed through New Year's Eve into New Year's Day. I was full of hope, aspirations, resolutions, expectations that the worst was over and that things could only get better.

The New Year celebration on board had been great. The wind had settled to around 20 knots from a west-south-west direction. With two reefs in the main and a small headsail, I felt the worst was over.

Now it was time to recover. Cape Horn would be my next big rounding, 7,000 miles or so to the east. The self-steering was working but the software had one small glitch where it would switch off. I had to react quickly to avoid going out of control.

Dramatic New Year's Day

One moment and life was great; then in an instant it was shattered.

The mast and complete rig exploded over the side.

After months of sailing and years of preparation, my whole life raced past.

And suddenly it was a fight for survival.

My God, there was a massive hole in the deck.

The seas were washing over the side.

It went from what had seemed a secure world to fighting for my life. There was no time to cry, to self-pity, not even to despair. That would all come later. Right then and there, I was lucky not to have been washed over the side.

Only a short time beforehand I'd made a little video interview for New Year and celebrated with a small bottle of champagne.

At that stage we were happily voyaging through the Pacific. It seemed the worst had passed. I made my traditional New Year resolutions. Ironically, I even recorded one, pledging to take less risk with my life. That was in the context of the previous 10 days. They had been tough. They shook me to the core. Here's an extract from the log showing just how shaken I had been.

"In business and throughout my life I have taken a lot of risks. But it has become too much. It has to stop or be less. I cannot continue like this. Yes, the risk enabled me to make enough money to buy this boat, to pursue the dream, to chase my adventure. But now I need to pull back. Enough is enough."

It started with an accidental gybe. The self-steering had turned off and quickly I jumped into the cockpit to get it going again — but too late; the boat inadvertently gybed and went on her side.

I released the runner to get her back and re-booted the steering; but I was struggling.

Crouched in the cockpit corner fighting with the rudder, I remember staring at the wind speed: 20 knots, then 25, then 30, then 35 and it kept rising. Fast.

I had read about this phenomenon but this was the first time to experience wind rising dramatically with little notice in this part of the Pacific.

The entire rig went. It blasted over the side. The load was so great, it could not take it any longer. It was like an explosion. There was a radial change in the boat's movement. It was chaos. The mast remained connected to the boat with more than 80 lines coming into the cockpit alone. The bigger risk was the stump of the mast hammering like a loose cannon into the boat. If left to its own devices it could punch a hole in the hull.

There was no time to stop and contemplate.

I immediately found the emergency cutting equipment. Fighting the waves pouring over the side now the boat was stationary, I became Mr Slasher.

It would have been good to keep some rig and spars for a jury rig, but there was too much risk. The safest thing was to cut it all away.

It was a struggle for what seemed an eternity (probably 30 minutes) but eventually everything was clear. Then I covered the exposed deck and crawled below into three cold and wet sleeping bags.

And I cried.

And cried.

Physically exhausted, I gradually began to recover.

Like all major setbacks in life, I had little choice. I was lucky to be alive.

My next new goal would be to survive 24 hours and after that to get to land. The closest was about 180 miles north and west to South Island, New Zealand. We are talking about a seriously remote part of the world here.

To make matters worse, the propeller shaft for the auxiliary motor had seized with rigging. It would be impossible to dive in these swells to clear it. With not even a spinnaker pole, a boom or the stump of a mast, how would I get to land? Had I even wished to call the rescue services I was totally out of range.

The good news was I had enough food for a few months and the ability to make water.

But there was no escaping the grim reality. I had rolled the dice, was caught unawares, and had to accept the consequences. It should not have happened. Over the previous 55 days, we had sailed 13,153 nautical miles (more than 24,000 kilometres) through some of the worst weather imaginable.

I had overcome rigging issues, electrical problems and mental challenges. But losing the mast was something impossible to repair.

There was no escape from the facts.

Devastated I may have been but I had to accept what happened. This sort of sailing is all about living on the edge. Shit happens. I had a flashback to exactly two year's previous when, early New Year's Day, I'd put in that call to buy the boat.

Now?

Well, now my dream had been shattered.

Or so I thought.

The storm had passed.

It was a pregnant silence without the sound of the mast and rig.

It was eerie.

The seas had flattened but it was cold. I didn't know what to do. I remember chatting on the sat phone back home as if I was in the next room. Luckily (for safety reasons), the aerial was mounted aft and had not gone the way of the mast. So there I was with instant contact, yet miles from anywhere. It was cold; there were no sails to trim, lines to pull or work to be done.

There was a feeling of nothingness.

¶ ¶ ¶ ¶

On reflection, had I not made that fateful call at a New Year's party to Mike Golding to buy the Kilcullen Voyager, none of this would have happened.

I remember calling Mike. There and then we agreed the price and did the deal. Like marriage: for better or worse.

Now, exactly two years later, something terrible had happened. After mastering the boat, with a Transatlantic Race podium achieved, I'd qualified for the main event, sailed up and down to the Canaries, around Ireland and half way around the planet.

No wonder I was a bundle of emotion, trying to figure out what it all meant.

I was heartbroken and devastated.

LESSONS FROM CHAPTER 11
- When disaster happens, accept it, reconfigure new goals and go forward.
- Accidents happen when you least expect them; so be prepared.
- Be careful with New Year resolutions.

> *Back home, the disaster was
> big news too. It was much to my
> annoyance but that's the reality:
> disaster makes news. On a personal
> basis I was not keen to talk about it.*

Chapter 12
New Zealand

L OSING the mast was dramatic — and that is an understatement. From racing in the fast lane to suddenly being mastless meant the boat's movement changed dramatically. The constant rig noise was gone.

Totally alone, after crying, sleeping, then getting myself back together, the storm blew over and reality kicked me in the face.

From intense focus to complete my solo circumnavigation, my next target was to survive the first few minutes. Then the next few hours. Like life itself, it was simply a matter of re-setting my goals.

I determined to make for the nearest land in Otago Bay, New Zealand. Rescue services were way out of range, anyhow, but I decided not to even attempt to call them.

After getting myself into difficulties of my own free will, it was my responsibility to get out and not be a burden on anyone.

But without even a boom or mast stump and 180 miles from South Island how would I do that? Not easily — that's for sure.

Thanks to a suggestion from Marcus over the sat phone I connected spare long carbon battens as a sort of Indian wigwam tent and pitched each of the batten ends in the dagger-board cases.

Then I hung a headsail upside-down. It worked. Lo and behold, in the 20 knot favourable winds I managed to average 1.5 knots and to go as fast as 2.5 knots and sometimes three in the surges. It was a far cry from 20-plus a short time beforehand.

After a few days another storm came in, again from the south, so progress was good.

Fisherman Steve Little came out to tow me the last 20 miles, and up Otago Bay into Dunedin. In the dark he guided us past the outer Port Chambers. We would have berthed there but it did not have enough depth. Appropriately enough, I suppose, this was the same spot from which the famous Irishman Ernest Shackleton had left for the Antarctic 100 years previously.

Steve and his team were a welcome sight. Even more so since he and his wife, Jo, owned the Carey's Bay Inn pub. It also had accommodation. They kindly gave me a room over the bar, a blast of whiskey for a memorable welcome, and a hot bath.

Such was the novelty of my arrival and the lack of news in the area I was to become a tourist attraction during my time there. Thankfully my presence brought business to the pub too.

Me? I reckoned that, as I was not due home for several weeks, why rush things? Some family and friends had kindly offered to fly down — but there seemed little point.

My adventures made the front page lead story in several daily editions of the Otago Daily Times. In one major piece I was competing with headlines over concerns for some local penguins.

Back home, the disaster was big news too. It was much to my annoyance but that's the reality: disaster makes news. On a personal basis I was not keen to talk about it.

¶ ¶ ¶ ¶

Through the Spirit of New Zealand charity which was linked with our Atlantic Youth Trust Charity I came to know Steve Fisher. He was the chairman who connected with BBQ Bill (Tony Cummins) and his extraordinary family.

After three days, when suitably recovered in the warm hospitality of the pub (and after riding a bike borrowed from Steve) I knew, though I told no one, I simply had to complete the trip.

I just had to finish.

How, or when, still had to be worked out.

Tony Cummins immediately picked up on the vibe. We built a great friendship.

Some years back, he and four others had been shipwrecked. He was the only survivor after being washed up on a beach. He also knew he had to go back to sea. Devastated, of course, but he felt he had to get another boat and go again. So he built an impressive steel yacht in his back garden and he called it "Wife" for reasons best known to himself.

He is a character. I remember, much to the embarrassment of his wife and family, as we sat over dinner at his home, he said: "The Kiwis like to party on Saturday nights and sow our wild oats. Then, on Sunday, we go to church to pray for crop failure".

Truth to tell I was honoured to be invited to their home and to experience some semblance of normal family living after so long alone at sea.

¶ ¶ ¶ ¶

Also alongside me in Dunedin was Le Souffle du Nord, another boat in the Vendée Race, skippered by Toma Ruyant which had almost broken in half.

In itself this was a dramatic story. Thomas was lucky to have made it to land in South Island. Terrified from the experience, he had headed back home to France.

Stuart McLachlan, who became a good friend and helper, had saved the boat and was looking after it. Stuart is one of those people who has a 'can-do' attitude, can fix anything and make things happen.

He had been in Galway for the Volvo Ocean Race. He ran an ocean racing yacht in Chicago on the Great Lakes and would go anywhere. But Dunedin was his home.

As far as I was concerned the French boat amounted to love

at first sight. My boat was holed with no mast: Toma's yacht was broken up but had a mast. It seemed to make perfect sense.

However, the syndicate owners could not decide. One problem had to do with disagreement with the insurance company on whether the boat would be written off or not.

As you probably know by now, if I have one personal failing it is not knowing when or how to give up. It took me several months to take on this new love but I never gave up.

In the meantime, helped by BBQ Bill and Paddy O'Connor, I found a temporary mast in a yard. The owner kindly agreed to donate it. Tony and many volunteers helped.

So then I set out from Otago Bay up along the coast.

The plan, initially, was to sail to Auckland, more than 1,000 miles up around the coast and to get another mast there so I could finish.

However, Christchurch seemed a more realistic option. So we set sail with a temporary mast and a musical send-off from the quayside in Dunedin.

Δ Day 74 — Final, Final, Final log... for the moment

This is really the last log until Kilcullen Voyager Version II continues some time in the future. Unless, of course, the skipper gets locked up on returning to Ireland and the keys get lost...)

Our Log 11 days ago on making a landfall in Otago was the most recent. Since I have learned that 'never' is a word never to use, this update is for those who have been curious about what has been happening on our odyssey since falling off the Vendée radar.

Most of all, this log is to say thanks to many and acknowledge the wonderful support. My God it has been a whirlwind. So here goes.

Not long after getting ashore, in Otago, the planning

started. Landing in this remote location, knowing no one, has been an adventure and a challenge all on its own. In the context of life itself, it's a 'first-world problem' and we are lucky to be alive; lucky to live.

Now here we are, a week later; we have a new 'old' temporary mast and we have made a landfall at Timaru up the coast. And tomorrow, Thursday at dawn, we set out for Christchurch. All last week as we prepared in Otago, it was daily headline news in the local media. Not a lot happens there; but they are great people.

More than 100 came to send us off. There was fanfare, including an Irish folk band and a barbecue, courtesy of BBQ Bill.

Our departure is possible thanks to the fisherman they call 'Rambo' (Steve Little) who towed us in (we did not call rescue services if you remember) and his wife Jo. I stayed above their pub at Carey's Bay.

Another champion was Tony Cummins — aka Barbeque Bill. Others who helped include Stuart McLachlan, Martin Balch, Blair McNabb and many, many more.

Let me also mention Paddy O'Connor, the Roscommon emigrant to Cork, formerly of the Irish Naval Service, incredibly skilled and an old friend. He happened to be on the South Island at the time. He was fantastic.

And now the Kilcullen has a mast and sails, complete with a VHF aerial, navigation lights and an AIS safety transmitter.

Moving up along the coast is akin to having a lawnmower engine on a Formula One car.

We started in fair winds and went straight out to sea, making an amazing five to six knots. A day later the forecast was less favourable. There were rapidly moving weather systems off the coast.

Our choice was to go right offshore, considered safer

until the winds became more favourable, to get us to Christchurch; or go to an intermediary port, Timaru.

Truckloads of kelp bladder-type seaweed and the unfavourable forecast, made the decision for us. During the night we sailed through a massive clump of seaweed which wrapped around the keel and the sail drive on our auxiliary motor, jamming the shaft.

Disabled again with no engine, it took us almost two days to make it to Timaru without assistance or calling for help. Timaru is a commercial port with massive container ships and few small-boat facilities. Early morning, we rounded the lead breakwater, coming dangerously close to the rocks. We anchored inside to get a tow onto a berth later by the harbour launch.

David Tee kindly dived to free the staggering amount of seaweed around the keel.

Suitably rested and with the wind moving into the west and south-west, we sail north for Christchurch at dawn on Friday morning, 20th January.

This is really the last log for while as your humble skipper will stop, get back to work and a sort of normal life — if that is possible.

That will either be on Kilcullen Voyager 1 or II (another boat). And it will depend on costs and repairs to finish the adventure and circumnavigation.

Of course there is always the chance, as I outlined at the start, that I will get locked up beforehand.

Once again, thanks for sharing the adventure.

Thanks for the wonderful support and interest.

The sea is a bit like being in the ring with an immortal boxer or Duracell bunny. He keeps chipping away until you're knocked down but you always get up and go to fight another round. Until no more.

Merci.

LESSONS FROM CHAPTER 12

↗ In life you are sometimes in the ring and getting knocked down but you have to keep getting up to fight another round.

↗ If you party and sow wild oats on a Saturday night, be sure to go to Church on Sunday to pray for crop failure.

↗ You may love an idea at first sight and decide to go for it, however it can take time to woo the other party. So persevere when you know it's right for both.

↗ Formula One cars don't work well with lawnmower engines.

*I was on edge. There was a lot
of pressure. It was my absolute
focus to complete what I had started.
As I'd spent all my budget and
more, it was a case of selling assets
(and my children's inheritance)
to get the money to finish.*

Chapter 13
Reality Kicks In

BACK in Ireland reality and depression kicked in. I had left South Island and the Kiwi summer. I'd made many friends and re-established old contacts. So it was a case of getting back to work. Or so I thought.

It was really a state of limbo between two lives and two adventures. While I could have dined out on the disaster all year, doing the rounds of talk shows, TV etc, I went to ground and turned most of it down.

The exceptions were a great night out at the RIYC with friends, and the tennis club, and a night in Galway which was a bit of a disaster (even my good friend and cousin Brian Lynch fell asleep).

The Lady Nicola, to my pleasant surprise, took me back. I was no longer alone. Sometimes you need to be away to fully appreciate family and friends. It was also great to see my new grandchild Feile, born just before I'd crossed the Equator on the way out.

But lurking all the while in the background was the desire to finish. It flitted around my sub-conscious and hindered kick-starting the rest of my life.

Firstly, I learned that the Souffle du Nord people thought me a little crazy with my proposal. Nothing unusual there. François Bouy, who led the ownership syndicate, admitted later they did not take me seriously at first.

I was on edge. There was a lot of pressure. It was my absolute focus to complete what I had started. As I'd spent all my budget and more, it was a case of selling assets (and my children's inheritance) to get the money to finish.

I was driven. I simply had to do it. I could not wait for the next Vendée.

The objective to sail solo around the world — even if just with one stop — was now driving me to the point where logic had no logic.

There was a lot of discussion. Permutations and combinations were explored. It seemed the partnership could not materialise. In the end I decided to acquire Rick Wilson's 'Great American IV' (GA4) to complete the trip. Assisted by Marcus, we did the costings and made initial plans to ship her to New Zealand. Then just before closing GA4, the Souffle du Nord people came back to explore the idea further. Regardless, I decided to proceed with GA4 since I had shaken hands with Rick.

Just before the delivery of my new boat to Port La Forêt, I got a positive email. The idea we first proposed in the Tír na Óg Irish Pub in Lille, northern France was gaining legs.

I went straight to Lille and the deal was closed before midnight at François' home in the Normandy countryside with other members of his board. In the process we made some wonderful friendships.

It was all agreed. Le Souffle du Nord would merge with Team Ireland and both teams would be one. I would be the nominated skipper, as their ambassador, to complete the sole circumnavigation.

It would be a win-win. My original hull was sold to Michael Dedjeaus of Mer Agitée; GA4 would be sold to Stewart Hosford of 5 West and my team would own Le Souffle du Nord with a complex hand-over protocol.

What a deal and solution.

Yes, the name was a mouthful: "Le Souffle du Nord Kilcullen Team Ireland." But we had a boat. That was all that mattered.

It was to be totally rebuilt in Christchurch by Davie Norris. Then we hatched a plan to sail around New Zealand up to Auckland in November as part of our preparation. And back to Dunedin in January. Both trials would be with a crew, but after that I'd be setting out solo to finish what was started.

¶ ¶ ¶ ¶

So, in the end I would have used two boats in the successful solo circumnavigation. It might be worth giving you a little information on them at this stage.

Both are in the 'IMOCA' Class. That is that they are designed and built according to an international rule. This rule specifies the maximum length to be 60 feet; they must be self-righting and fulfil a range of weight and strength criteria with a maximum mast height.

Boat One — the Kilcullen Voyager

This is an Owen Clarke and was built originally in New Zealand in 2007. Formerly owned by Mike Golding, she lost her mast on New Year's Day 2017 and was holed. The hull was sold and shipped back to France where she has since been rebuilt

Kilcullen Le Souffle du Nord: Boat 2

This is a VVP design and was built in France in 2008. She was owned by the Le Souffle du Nord syndicate and sailed by Thomas Ruyant. She broke almost in half after hitting either a container or a whale, and barely made it back to New Zealand. She was then rebuilt and renamed when both the Irish and French Team merged with me as skipper and Ambassador of both Around the World Projects

¶ ¶ ¶ ¶

Among those joining us for the voyage around New Zealand would be Joan Mulloy, who had asked me to help her enter the

Vendée Race. I admired her ambition, drive and ability. As a trained young engineer she had dropped her professional career to follow her dream as a professional sailor. Her west-of-Ireland background was similar to mine. She had even captained the college sailing club I'd founded with her uncle Brian Lynch — my schoolmate, cousin and friend.

LESSONS FROM CHAPTER 13

↗ If you don't seek, you don't get, as I discovered in looking for part of Le Souffle Du Nord.

↗ Sometimes you need to be away to fully appreciate your family and friends.

Chapter 14
Auckland, Here We Come

BACK in New Zealand, with a totally re-built boat, refreshed and recharged, it was magic to get to sea again. Ah! The thrill of experiencing the freedom.

This was a down-payment for the intense work and preparation for my sole goal. With the ship's log restarted, we set out for Auckland with a tourist stop in Wellington where we were to visit all the Irish pubs.

△ Log — Act II

This is the bit in the middle. We're circumnavigating New Zealand and this comes from off Kaikoura, South Island.

ACT III will start in January when I will be honoured to set out as ambassador for SDN on board Kilcullen Voyager to complete our circumnavigation to Les Sables d'Olonne. That would be to unofficially finish the Vendée Globe for two teams, risking Cape Horn and the Southern Ocean without support.

It's calm now. We are about 15 miles from the coast. The blackness of the night is starting to lighten in anticipation of the spring sunrise. There is little wind as we prepare to cross the Cook Strait which divides New Zealand's North and South Islands. At sea again, it seems circumnavigating New Zealand, has become a modest little challenge in the context of completing our lap of the planet. It's a planet whose oceans never cease to amaze and humble us.

It's all still a bit surreal. It was like yesterday, on board the Kilcullen Voyager, powering towards Cape Horn that my dream was shattered. All of a sudden it was 'wham', no mast and a new goal: to survive. Then Otago Bay a week later, a temporary mast to Christchurch, the merging and marriage of two teams. Everything moved as if in a dream, or should I say nightmare?

Now, re-invented, I again recall the words of Samuel Beckett:

'Perhaps my best years are gone....
but I wouldn't want them back.
Not with the fire in me now.'

¶ ¶ ¶ ¶

Earlier in the week it had been edgy. Getting the boat out of Davie Norris's yard in Christchurch, blocking off the highway and successful launching in Lyttelton Harbour had all been a challenge.

The weather was bad through launch and sailing trials; it blew hard. Happily the boat is in great shape — in fact, the rebuild has made her almost better than new. She is certainly stronger — and reinforced where it matters.

I was nervous as I departed. That had nothing to do with surviving a thank-you night out with all our new Christchurch friends and Michael Keane (Sligo) of The Claddagh Pub.

Amanda Norris, who worked on the boatbuilding with Viki Moore, now a new Council Member of the New Zealand Yachting Association representing the South Island, braved the sharp spring wind to see us off.

And our romantic French team members (they do like their Guinness) left their girlfriends behind.

Our greatest concern in the light winds has been bumping into whales as we pass through the Kaikoura Bay area. This is world famous as a meeting and breeding ground for giant sperm, humpback, pilot blue and southern right whales. Keeping a constant lookout is vital.

We have five people on board here off South Island NZ: two French teammates Pierre-Antoine Tesson and Maxim Buoy from Le Souffle du Nord. Then there is Stuart McLachlan, the brilliant KIWI sailor in the middle and Joan Mulloy. Meanwhile as ever your skipper is happy at sea where passing the test of being a real Irishman is a doddle (the one who never goes to bed the same day he gets up).

After a pit stop in Wellington, we got to Auckland the following week with a 35/40 knot gale up our stern. We shot across the Bay of Plenty, over the top after negotiating the Eastern Cape — our 'Cape Horn'. Prior to that, it was a hard upwind slog from Wellington. IMOCA 60s are not happy sailing into the wind and big seas. Their crews are even less happy.

Now we're almost halfway around the two massive islands and many weather systems. The Kiwi circumnavigation, which we will now complete by sailing to Dunedin, is a mini-diversion on our way back to complete our 'humming bird and Irish mission'.

At times parts of New Zealand, especially in the south, can be sub-Antarctic and sub-tropical. Their storms would make the west-coast-of-France winter gales seem like a children's tea party, such is their fierce and dramatic nature.

The leg to Auckland had some drama. It included a crash gybe in darkness which smashed the traveller car. However, we have recovered and it was a valuable lesson: these are fragile boats and we are fragile. The ocean knows no emotion other than fury. And it is indifferent to our fate.

We were greeted on arrival by a group of Kiwi girls. They were clearly attracted to our two young Le Souffle du Nord crewmen, Maxime and Pierre.

However, their older skipper may have cramped their style by talking to their mothers.

'And to the ship that goes
.... The wind that blows
..... And the lass who loves a sailor' (in every port)

So this is our last log — I think — until we sail again to complete our voyage around NZ to Dunedin and then back to finish in Les Sables.

But first, your skipper travels back to Europe and looks forward to meeting all in Dublin on 30th November. This will include the launch of our Schools Adventure Programme by Minister Mary Mitchell O'Connor, a lunch, and workshop on using ocean adventure in education, a reception hosted by the French Ambassador to Ireland.

And then a night out in Dublin.

¶ ¶ ¶ ¶

The Atlantic Youth Trust looked at 16 countries to survey their youth maritime development models. As it happens the New Zealand one was the best, where the Spirit of Adventure Trust runs the Spirit of NZ, a 45-metre tall ship.

So in January we have a group of youth taking a 10-day voyage from 6th to 15th starting, and finishing, in Auckland. Then from the 14th to 16th we have an official visit to meet the NZ charity trustees and see their youth development model at first hand. This will be valuable in developing the trust, not just as a north/south island of Ireland youth project, but also a European one.

Unrelated, but parallel to the voyage we will have the first gathering of Irish Hospitality Global bringing together an association for Irish pub and restaurant owners in New Zealand as part of our global network.

¶ ¶ ¶ ¶

The plan then is for our team to depart Auckland in January for Dunedin — thus completing a circumnavigation of New Zealand.

Thanks for sharing the mission, vision and adventure. Let the dreamers dream!

LESSONS FROM CHAPTER 14

↗ When you get the chance to do something again, grab it with both hands.

↗ Sometimes when things go wrong, the first rung back is to recover. Like life, the ocean knows no pity and you shouldn't expect any.

It was magic, after 24 hours travelling, to land in between the mountain ranges. It was straight out of Lord of the Rings.

Chapter 15
New Year, New Start

A S I've already outlined, I decided to write this book on the New Year's flight to New Zealand as my son Cormac and I rang in 2018 at 35,000ft.

I am writing the book not just to chart the journeys, euphoria, trials and tribulations but to share what I've personally learned from the adventure.

It posed a challenge I was privileged, and lucky, to be able to undertake.

Yes, there is also a bit of vanity and pride in being published. There is always the hope it might fire someone's imagination — and sell copies. That wish/hope/dream comes from a time when I devoured every adventure and business book I could find. My thinking was: If anybody else can do it, so can I.

In a selfish way, writing about the voyage gives it all a finality; it allows me to leave it behind and move on with the business of living. Even if nobody bothers to read it, at least it's done. And it is something in which I hope my family will take pride. My grandchildren and their children's children may wonder what that dude was up to in pushing the boundaries.

For sure, we'll all be a long time dead.

Before joining the boat, Cormac and I diverted to Queenstown in the south island for a week of daddy-son time. It is one of the most incredible parts of the country. Our arrival was staggering. It was magic, after 24 hours travelling, to land in between the mountain ranges. It was straight out of The Lord of the Rings.

Steve Fisher kindly loaned me his cottage and jeep. We had a ball. It included bungee jumping, jet boats and sheep-shearing. We even went prospecting for gold in the mountains. For my son, it made real the story of his great-great grandfather Cormac. That was the man who had crossed the Rockies, made his way to California, to Klondike and — unusual for the time — managed to return home with enough gold to afford a pub, a wife and family.

Anyway, a week later we got back to Auckland to join the boat and team for a busy period of preparation. Superbly organised by Rob Elliot of Lemongrass Productions in partnership with the Spirit of Adventure Trust, we had a great Irish breakfast at the Viaduct where SDN Kilcullen and the Spirit of New Zealand were based.

It was linked with a crew change and the Irish youth exchange which was a great success. Friends travelled from Ireland — including David Beattie, a fellow trustee of the charity. It is our hope to replicate the Kiwi model in Ireland. Indeed, not ones to waste an opportunity, we had a unique and first gathering of Irish pub owners in the country under the Irish Hospitality Global banner. It was a busy time and was covered on national TV.

Cormac's sister Saoirse also arrived. Their plan was to go venturing while SDN Kilcullen set out for Dunedin to be the ultimate start point. Here Billy Walsh was a great help; he has been a great friend in Auckland. A professional banker in Ireland, he migrated and held a senior executive position with the Bank of New Zealand.

Billy lined up a Maori priest and elders to come bless the boat before sailing. It was deep and spiritual, reflecting the people's close links with the elements and nature. The Maori chief said New Zealand had taken us in, looked after us and was now sending us on our way.

The dramatic downpour and rain added to the sense of occasion and ceremony; the chief said it was a good omen.

For us it was all great fun as we played and sang through a lovely send-off. The 'us' comprised me, the boat and French teammates Maxime Bouy, Pierre-Antoine Tesson, together with Peadar Gill and Nin O'Leary representing the Aran Islands and the kingdom of Cork respectively. The 'extras' were for my final shakedown voyage to Dunedin. This would be useful for preparations and safety around the New Zealand coast. After that I am all alone to 'unofficially' finish the Vendée.

Δ Log

Sailing out the Hauraki Gulf with the dramatic skyline of Auckland astern we had 30 to 35 knot gale force winds on the nose. However, with three reefs in the main and small J3 headsail we powered upwind. That first night at sea was tough and warm. But summer was swiftly supplanted by the cold ocean.

It is also difficult to transit from shore to life on the ocean wave. You are constantly rolling in every direction imaginable, bruising, banging and even the simplest of tasks take planning and agility. But that's the magic and the challenge of how our bodies can adapt and be taken from their sedentary settled ways.

We then had a difficult decision around what route to take: North about or South about. In the end expediency, prudence and safety made the decision for us, much and all as we would have liked to have gone 'over the top'.

¶ ¶ ¶ ¶

Back in Dunedin old friendships were re-established.

BBQ Bill, aka Tony Cummins, and his family gave us a great welcome. The Otago Times was all over the story again — though I preferred not to make much fuss. We again stayed at the Carey's Bay Inn and had a small send-off party.

First it was an emotional goodbye for Saoirse and Cormac at the airport. And suddenly I was alone.

LESSONS FROM CHAPTER 15

↗ We'll be a long time dead, so do the things that you want
— live your dreams

↗ Parting is a sweet sorrow, especially when you are all
alone on the high seas.

Chapter 16
At Sea To Infinity

CROSSING the international dateline took a long time. Then all of a sudden it was upon us. The GPS went from 179.59 E to peak for a second at 180 and then 179.59 W. That's really when the long countdown to the finish began. It was an emotional, unreal moment. It took me back to the future. Imagine: what was Sunday 28th became Saturday 27th January, 2018.

And, sure, what is time?

It stretches in my mind from Albert Einstein's theory of relativity to my own inability to understand the concept of infinity.

I cannot grasp it. It defies logic. There is no logic to the logic. It is beyond imagination. To imagine what we cannot imagine? Is that not the abstract of God? If not, I'm sure he'd have something to say about it.

Δ Log Day 2 (77) Act III

It's really mighty to be under way. Sailing around the Kiwi coast to Auckland and back South again was an ambitious 2,500 miles but we did it. It was an adventure all of its own. The boat was proven and our shore-side exchange with the Spirit of Adventure and Atlantic Youth Trusts was a great success.

To represent Le Souffle du Nord and Kilcullen Team Ireland, it is an honour to be charged with finishing both missions. It's also a big responsibility. When I look ahead to the enormity of the Pacific Ocean it does not feel real. But it is.

Yet in the humble context of time and relativity what is it?

Now I am all on my own.

The first night it blew up to 30 knots and it was hard going. It was a massive adjustment. The more I think about it, the more anxious I have become over what lies ahead. Powering east and south, it's already cold and getting colder.

Covering more than 400 miles in a day was a good start. Or perhaps not, since in reality it was two days. Approximately 240 miles in the first 24 hours. We have just passed between the Bounty islands to the north and the Antipodes islands to the south.

The former seem like nothing more than a clump of rocks; the latter volcanic islands look interesting. The main island is an important UNSECO listed bird shelter about 20km square.

The island group was first charted in 1800 by Captain Henry Waterhouse. In 1803 his brother-in-law George Bass was granted a fishing monopoly for the area.

Bass sailed from Sydney to the south that year and was never heard of again. However, his information about the large population of fur seals led to a sealing boom in the region from 1805 to 1807.

At one time there was a battle between American and British-led gangs. And a single cargo of more than 80,000 skins, one of the biggest shipped from Australasia, was sold in Canton for one pound sterling a skin. That's a multimillion-dollar return in modern terms. After 1807, sealing was occasional and cargoes small — no doubt because the animals had been all but exterminated.

And now leaving the Antipodes astern, sailing into the night of Saturday (Sunday just a few miles behind) with the wind gusts to 30 knots, I take from the words of Sean O'Casey:

'An' as it blowed an' blowed
I often look up into the sky
An' asked myself the question -
What is the stars what is the stars?'

Δ Log Day 5 (78) Act III

With more than 1,000 miles sailed since Dunedin, I am still looking back. The 12,000 ahead are too much to contemplate. But I am changing. Earlier today, feeling the isolation, I shouted and roared and walked the decks.

Who cares?

I don't matter. I am just a drop in the ocean. The problem is that I am distressingly sane; everybody else is mad. I state this as not only being a fact, but the truth.

Thanks to the wonderful update from Sylvie. She kindly described the skipper's log as being akin to 'finding a bottle in the sea' and reported the launch of our collective challenge of '13,000 miles for 13,000 smiles'.

Already for Le Project Imagine there is a way for people to respond to and document their little, big, actions for each mile we sail. It's wonderful.

The first application Sylvie reported is about one association wishing to promote the inclusion of young people with disabilities through sport. It seeks two volunteers to supervise groups of one-to-three children one hour a week for indoor football sessions. Another wants to return to Brittany to kiss his grandmother before she dies.

¶ ¶ ¶ ¶

So alone, I feel the sheer vastness and isolation. It's humbling. Since departing the Otago in New Zealand, I have not seen a solitary ship or any trace of humanity.

That is apart from the omnipresent magnificent albatross seabirds who once helped us save a life.

I become more afraid and nervous as time progresses. Each wave, each race around the deck, each activity, is a risk. Doing nothing is not an option. It's constant.

And while I can be really alone on the ocean, it is also possible for a fellow human to be totally alone and lonely in the company of thousands.

But this is living on the edge.

And the sight of the albatrosses, time and time again brought back memories of our crewman Willie. He was with us on the maxi when we sailed the Whitbread Around the World Race many years ago.

Unexpectedly and in an instant, he was gone overboard. A sagging spinnaker line caught him off guard and swept him over. In my view it's healthy to keep reminding myself of this and to always be on high alert. The motto is: Be fearful and ready to expect the unexpected.

As we were moving fast in the big seas, I remember how quickly we lost sight of Willie that day even though we'd quickly moved to slash sheets etc.

As one of the 16 on board I will never forget the emotion. A friend and companion gone; just gone. It was the albatross who saved his life.

Right now I look astern and see some hovering.

They are extraordinary birds. They can fly more than 1,000k a day and generally follow anything that moves in the southern Ocean — one of the few places where they are found.

The wingspans are the largest of any bird and exceed 340cm (11.2ft). Gliding on and with the prevailing winds they regularly fly around the bottom of the world.

The day that Willie disappeared the big birds followed him and not our yacht as soon as he was overboard. They broke off and hovered over Willie. If they had not it is unlikely we would have found him in time. But they guided us and we got him back on board. As can happen he was in a state of torpor. First you shiver; then it's hypothermia and your eyes glaze over — the final stage before death.

It was a close call. The albatrosses hovered all the time.

The more I researched them the more fascinated I became. They usually partner for life; seldom divorce and most live for 50 years or more. One, named Wisdom, which was ringed in 1956 as a mature adult hatched another chick in February 2017, thereby making her at least 66 years old. She is the oldest confirmed wild bird as well as the oldest banded bird in the world.

Δ Log, Day 9, Act III

The last two days have been awful. They have been dominated by two intensive 12-hour working days using all the available daylight. Going nowhere, repairing battens and other items that went wrong. Murphy's Law had a good outing.

Happily, Cape Horn edges closer. Only 3,000 miles to go. Despite what seemed like two major setbacks, we are back on track. After some sleep and recovery time, we're powering along the bottom of a gentle high-pressure zone over the bottom of our planet.

Weather routing is pointing us further south — to roll along the top of a depression. However, it's colder down there. While slower, I am not bothered and reckon we can still make the target to finish in 60 days. But with Murphy's Law on call you never know.

Essentially there was a small glitch in the NKE sophisticated HD self-steering system. It would randomly stop working. Before setting sail we had the KIWI agent investigate. He managed to relieve me of 500 dollars to learn he did not understand the system and could not fix it. The French manufacturer could not solve it either (by phone or online) but regardless we decided to sail. It was a calculated risk and we had a good back-up.

The HD was working really well. And then, while feeling confident I left it on while taking a nap. It was my error of judgment. The wind piped up and it went off course. We had a spectacular crash gybe — breaking three battens in the process. But any risk to the mast was avoided.

¶ ¶ ¶ ¶

On the ocean, rolling around in cramped space was physically demanding — a task that even on land would be tough for one person. First I had to get the sail down and extract the battens: a major exercise. Using a powerful mobile hand drill, the repair was awkward and messy, with carbon dust getting in everywhere. Then getting the battens back in was a huge test.

I am generally fit but almost every part of my body was pulled and tugged in several directions. Now all my bits ache. It's painful to move but I am in recovery mode. I would never have thought I could do it but it's amazing what you can do when you have to. It was a proud moment when I got the sail and engine safely under way again.

¶ ¶ ¶ ¶

Also on board we have a pet monkey. Adolf, as he is named, has taken on a Gestapo personality. He's with the gentle little teddy bear from Steve Fisher of the Spirit of Adventure Trust and the devious Paddy the Leprechaun from Dublin Duty Free.

Though he's only a stuffed toy, Adolf is the monkey on

my back. Maybe he is on François' and Sylvian's back too with Le Souffle du Nord as our joint mission to complete the Vendée course continues apace.

Δ Log, Day 11, Act III

With the South Pacific Residents Association today we celebrated Waitangi Day — February 6th. Our chairman considered it fitting in view of us being halfway between Chile (which hosts Cape Horn some 2,500 miles ahead) and New Zealand 2,500 miles astern.

As we make solid progress the chairman also passed a motion that the skipper should improve his French. The reason is that many of our 'back ups' on board are in French. So to run the boat and fulfil my duties I need that beautiful language. It would also be useful to support the great future plans and vision for Le Souffle du Nord where, when Sylvian and François get going, the pensioners will cast off their walking sticks and dance in the streets of Lille with joy.

To this day, I regret being a bad boy and having to leave our French class at school. Bad students had to go to the Commerce class.

Had Napoleon not gone east and his troops not frozen to death en route to Moscow, he might have come to Ireland. Then we would all speak French and eat more cheese. Instead we speak English and are so politically well balanced we have chips on both shoulders.

Central to today's celebration on board is that we have had the benefit of a ritual Maori blessing before departing New Zealand. And we carry spiritual symbols of this with Pounamu stones for home and with the stones 'Roommate' or 'Tears of Joy' (specially given to me by the Maori chief in Auckland before departing).

1) Focus on where you want to go

2) Freedom to be what you want to be

3) Fun, life is good.

As we celebrate there are few, if any, more remote spots on the planet. The closest islands are the tiny Picterns to the north and land — Antarctica — some 1,000 miles south.

And so the merging of the South Pacific with the Indian and South Atlantic Residents Association, Waitangi seemed like a natural as a celebration day. Worldwide, this has become New Zealand Day.

¶ ¶ ¶ ¶

It marks the founding document of the country — the famous signing of the treaty between the British Crown and more than 40 Maori chiefs at Waitangi, in the Bay of Island, north of Auckland on 6th February 1840.

The day, symbolic politically throughout New Zealand, has also been used as a beacon of protest by Maori activists about treaty injustices. This is a side of the country we do not see much about.

¶ ¶ ¶ ¶

Back in the nautical world, the Americas Cup is hugely symbolic. As is the amazing achievement of winning it. When in Auckland, as guests of the Royal New Yacht squadron (holders of the Cup), we were horrified to learn about a Maori activist gaining access and almost smashing the Cup to pieces. Happily, it was rebuilt by the original jewellers (dating from 1850 and security is like Fort Knox).

On board in my real 'unreal' world, progress has been steady. We have been on the same tack-and-sail combination for several days. A steady westerly wind blows constantly between 15 and 20 knots. Each day merges through overcast skies and drizzle with solid progress and no drama. I've developed a routine on board for this second week, following the trials, tribulations, damage and successful repairs in Week One.

To round off today's log and Waitangi Day, the skipper and entire council of the resident's association dined out at the best restaurant on board. I had a steak, medium rare on a stone with mushrooms, onions, fresh vegetables and, of course, chips.

Ahhh!, if only such a scenario was true.

From the words of Thomas Moore, who was told by his clergyman that Heaven punishes desires as much as deed:

'And, if wishing damns us, you and I
Are damned to all our heart's content:
Come, then, at least we may enjoy
Some pleasure for our punishment.'

¶ ¶ ¶ ¶

Not long after I sent that log I got a shock. The boom had come off the gooseneck. It was not broken — just unscrewed. Without it, the main could not function. While it was not serious damage, the physical challenge of getting it back on was massive. I was exhausted.

Δ Log, Day 14, Act III

I am pleased I solved the gooseneck problem. We were faced with a difficult choice. One was to go north over the top of a vicious looking low-pressure system. Or south around the bottom. Either way it would be a slog since the wind was predominantly east and north east — our general direction of travel. Cape Horn is ever so slowly getting closer and there appears to be harmony between the three Residents Association groups who merged into one.

Time will tell.

It looks as if the southerly option we've taken will work since the low has moved faster and deeper than expected. Also, being slower in the headwinds allows it to run before us. Going south is also colder. My fingers freeze a little while punching out this log (which I don't feel like doing but it's a regular discipline). Punters say this is madness — so be it. But it's desperately disciplined and you need to be seriously sane to express your madness.

Now starting our third week at sea, I am never away from the edge. Day after day, 24/7, or even 25/8, there is constant movement and risk.

There is always work to be done on these incredibly sophisticated boats refined for one man to operate. It's most definitely a love-hate relationship. It's massively isolated. I'm alone — but not lonely.

Progress has not been good. I found the boom had disconnected from the mast in a routine check. The swivel stainless fitting had unwound. It was two hours before dark and despite dropping the mainsail, darkness won in the struggle to get it fixed and the boom back in position. I was exhausted and went to bed — if you can call it that as I was crouched on the navigator's seat.

But it's amazing what rest and a fresh dawn brought. A new approach: unbolt the mast fitting, reconnect the stainless fitting (fortunately the screw thread was only a little damaged). Then a series of four sets of block and tackle to gradually leverage the boom gooseneck into the right position and it was problem solved.

After that there was no wind for almost 24 hours. It was dark; the sails clattered and we rolled in the swell. Then, within five minutes it went suddenly to gale force 35 knots. That made it a struggle to get the boat under control without damage. This was accomplished but not without shock to my system.

All of this, I might add, was reported for consultation with the executive of the Southern Ocean Residents Associations (SORA). The views and opinions of Adolf the Monkey, Paddy the Leprechaun and the Kiwi Spirited Teddy Bear were confusing.

¶ ¶ ¶ ¶

It has been a lifetime's work for me to bring ideas, community projects, companies and people together. I am proud to have been able to manage (not always successfully) the different personalities, beliefs, expectations and socio-economic backgrounds.

Happily, all is running smoothly now that the South Atlantic, Indian Ocean and South Pacific Residents Associations have merged and become SORA.

From here Cape Horn beckons.

As with the Atlantic meeting the Indian around the Cape of Good Hope and then the transition to the Pacific south of New Zealand, change brings turbulence.

So let's see what the next two weeks have in store. Hopefully they'll sail us into home Atlantic waters.

Δ Log, Day 18, Act III

Dropping my main sail over and over I feel a bit like a sex maniac dropping his trousers all the time. Now the main is down again for the third time. It's a demanding exercise, manic stuff, but sadly no sex.

And for the past while, with only a headsail set, the wind has been steady at 25 to 30 knots from the west. And cold. We have been making good progress between 10 and 15 knots towards the elusive Cape Horn, which the Southern Ocean Residents Association seldom stop discussing.

Currently I feel detached from the so-called world, living in a small capsule. A disconnected bubble. However, the support I am getting is appreciated. There seems to be a ' head of steam' with Le Souffle du Nord and Project Imagine. Mile by mile, it's really encouraging. Likewise, in Ireland there is great progress with school activities and promoting the Atlantic Youth Trust.

I pulled the main down in a 40-knot squall when the repaired third batten had broken. Adding insult to injury, the batten, like a swordsman out of control, stabbed several holes in the sail. That gives you an idea of how violent the flogging was in the squall. Now it's a question of biding time and finding suitable weather to patch and hopefully away with the main again. Happily, in the strong westerlies, having no main does not seem to matter a hoot.

Previously I had to drop the main when a halyard became loose. With a heavy locking device at the end, it proceeded to wrap itself around everything aloft, including the outriggers.

It was simply safer to drop sail and climb up the mast and outrigger to solve it.

In many ways sailing without a mainsail is tedious in heavy conditions. However, it is much less stressful. There is no worry about involuntary gybes, damage or the boat going out of control. Instead you plonk along. Now it's so easy for gybes and so forth. Generally with the main, we do not gybe above 20 knots. Instead it means hardening up on the wind and doing 360, often difficult in big seas, but safer. And time rolls on.

With time, getting jet lag on a boat comes in slow motion. It takes so long it's akin to watching paint dry. Each day sailing east, the sun goes down earlier and I find it disorienting. From crossing the international dateline a few weeks back at the 180th we are now almost at 100 degrees. So rather than keep a 'ship's time' I work off GMT which means it gets dark around 14:30pm. And the sun rises around midnight.

¶ ¶ ¶ ¶

It is supposedly summer down here. If so I would hate to be here during winter. The cold is penetrating. Even with three layers of thermals, the only way to stay together is to pile on clothes and be religious about wearing oilskins on deck. Regardless, however, the damp and wet penetrates everywhere. And if it's not coming externally, internal body perspiration during activities also make my clothes wet. Needless to say the inner layers do not come off, and when they do, you don't want to be near.

However, I keep sane thanks to the regularity of food, cat napping, routine maintenance work on board and dreaming. Or does it keep me sane?

I'm not so sure. Last evening, while in the middle of a review of the day with the Residents Association, we had an unexpected visitor.

He was a British seaman who called himself Cape Horn Man and looked to be in his late twenties. He said he had fallen overboard on a passage. And because his body was never found he is locked in perpetual eternity, warning passing ship captains to take care.

My final thoughts are summarised in the final stanza of Invictus by William Ernest Henley.

The poem was kindly nominated by Bettina of the Project Imagine Team who is in charge of producing their films:

' It matters not how strait the gate,
How charged with punishments the scroll,
I am the master of my fate:
I am the captain of my soul.'

LESSONS FROM CHAPTER 16

↗ Be fearful and ready to expect the unexpected.

↗ It's amazing what you can do when you have to.

Chapter 17
Bring On Cape Horn

Δ Log, Day 23, Act III

Cape Horn ahead was a scary prospect. I was surfing along at almost 20 knots with just a small headsail as the wind approached 50 knots and the seas built. Each wave seemed bigger than the previous.

More disturbing was the fact the waves often came from different directions as the turbulent Atlantic clashed with the mighty Pacific.

This was the great meeting point of legend, folklore and a graveyard for many fine ships. It was also violent. My worry was about being swamped, swirled around out of control, somersaulted and de-masted.

But there was no going back as we plunged into the turbulence with the hope of coming out the other side.

Our rounding at 22:41hrs, 16th February 2018, exceeded all expectations.

As if by magic it seemed like we had entered the Garden of Eden — without Eve or any apple trees — soon after turning the corner. It warmed up, the winds became lighter, and the seas were flatter in the lee of Tierra del Fuego. Yet, down at the Horn, it was still howling. To boot, the South Atlantic Residents Association gave us an imaginary champagne reception.

The experience drove home the exceptional nature of Cape Horn. The Roaring 40s, the Howling 50s and the

Screaming 60s are the bands of latitude around the bottom of our plane where the winds and oceans roll from the west almost uninterrupted.

The winds are exacerbated at the Horn by the funnelling effect of the Andes and the Antarctic Peninsula. The waves also encounter an area of shallower water, which has the effect of making them shorter and steeper, thereby increasing the hazards. The area is notorious as well for rogue waves which can tower 30 metres (98ft) high. And of course there are the ice hazards.

The Cape was discovered and first rounded in 1616 by Dutchman Willem Schouten. He named it Kaap Hoorn after his home city of Hoorn in the Netherlands.

Drake Passage, south of the Horn, was discovered by accident in 1578 when Sir Thomas Drake was blown off course. He was on his way around the world through the Straits of Magellan — a passage further north through the bottom of Chile and Argentina.

And it was the Straits of Magellan that Joshua Slocum, the great American single-handed circumnavigator, negotiated. He was smart. I always recollect his narrative of anchoring at night in the straits with no guard against the local Indians. Instead he used thumbtacks — his secret weapon. He described how he woke suddenly in the middle of the night to screaming and roaring as the barefooted robbers discovered the painful hidden tacks.

For decades Cape Horn was a major milestone in the Clipper route by which sailing ships carried cargo around the world and for US ships going coast to coast.

Traditionally a sailor who had rounded Cape Horn was entitled to wear a gold-loop earring (in the left ear). He also earned the right to dine with one foot on the table. Incidentally, a sailor who had rounded the Cape of Good Hope could dine with both feet on the table.

The need for ships to round Cape Horn was massively reduced with the opening of the Panama Canal in 1914 and with the opening of transcontinental railways.

The Chilean navy maintain a station close by and it is part of Antarctica Chilean province. There are no trees. It rains 270 days of the year; average winds are close to gale force with 100-knot squalls.

One historic attempt is immortalised by the attempt of the HMS Bounty in 1788. The subsequent Mutiny on the Bounty was fictionalised. Bounty made only 85 miles of headway in 31 days of east-to-west sailing before giving up and going around Africa instead.

In fact the first small boat to sail around the Horn was said to be the 42-footer Saoirse, sailed by Limerick man Conor O'Brien. With three crew, he rounded it during his circumnavigation of the world between 1923 and 1925. The first to do it singlehanded was Argentina's Vito Dumas in 1942 on his 33-footer

Δ Log, Still Day 23

Wrapping up the Log, the Horn adventure for your skipper was an emotional turning point. I was euphoric after the tribulations of the vast Pacific over the past year in getting there.

On land, it was the equivalent of a good night out, making love, being with friends and helping someone make their world a better place.

Subsequently it was back to the reality of removing and repairing a massive mainsail. And getting this great ship, I have the honour to command, the 8,000 miles up the Atlantic to finish. Home boys, home.

Of the many stories of poets and adventurers telling of hazardous journeys around this iconic landmark I quote:

'One sight of such a coast is enough

To make a landsman dream for a week
About shipwrecks, peril and death'
(Charles Darwin)
' Cape Horn that tramples beauty into wreck
And crumples steel
And smites the strong man dumb'
(John Masefield)

Δ Log, 26, Act III

It was a major event — the skipper changed his socks.

And one of the largest cruise ships in the world, the Island Princess out of Bermuda, turned around on our account. And a deep sea trawler off Chile gave us a shock. We thought they were pirates.

And most important, the mainsail repairs have been completed.

Now we have no need to stop at the Falklands and are slowly beating north into headwinds up the South Atlantic.

The sock change came after three weeks on the same feet — night and day. I might almost say they hardened up and walked themselves, while being cheered and encouraged by the Southern Ocean Residents Association. While they gave good service, the sheer delight of wearing a fresh pair was almost erotic.

Which reminds me of a story, in poor taste, told by the President of the SORC at the sock-at-sea burial when the Nazi officer announced to his concentration camp prisoners that they would have a change of underwear:

"Camp 1 vill change vith camp 3"

"Camp 2 vill change vith camp 4"

Like them I have been wearing the same clothes all the time for warmth. I am also fairly certain the socks would not have qualified for the Souffle du Nord 'odd socks' charity fundraising campaign. So they were no loss when tossed over the side. Being biodegradable, the ocean will quickly absorb them.

This is unlike my other rubbish in two refuse sacks collected on board from living. This will be disposed of, and hopefully recycled, in some landfill.

Be that as it may, following the elation of rounding Cape Horn, it was back to work to execute repairs under almost ideal conditions. For almost two days we were becalmed off the coast of Tierra del Fuego.

The ocean was beautiful, rich in sea life with large clumps of drifting seaweed that snarled around the keel and rudders. The weed was difficult to remove; sailing the boat backwards helped.

And while not pretty, the mainsail repair looks solid. For one person it had been demanding to remove the sail from the boom and patch it. Effectively one of the broken battens went out of control in the 40- knot squall when I was dropping the main. Its sharp end punched two large, and eight small, holes in the sail.

Fortunately, the damage was not structural to the sail. After sewing the heavy sail together I put on several patches secured by Sycaflex, a powerful flexible adhesive.

It was another problem and another solution.

Through David Beattie, and then Russell Best, we had a kind introduction to the harbourmaster at Port Stanley in the Falklands. Fortunately, I managed to avoid stopping for repairs which has a different set of risks for a solo sailor in a 60-footer in a commercial port.

Also, within the 'Spirit of the Vendée' and finishing unofficially, I wanted, if at all possible, to remain self-contained and complete the repair on-board.

For many other reasons it would have been great to visit the Falklands and see how they are getting on since

Argentina grabbed them from the British in 1982. (Of course Margaret Thatcher quickly mustered an invasion task force to win them back two months later.)

Now, all these years later, the islands are self-governed while Britain provides Defence and Foreign Office representation.

The islands developed mostly as a shipping base and repair centre, some 350 miles from Cape Horn, before the Panama Canal opened in 1914. They had been in decline until the Argentinian invasion.

As we sailed north past the Falklands and up along the South American coastline, my collision alarm sounded on board early in the morning.

I could make out that a vessel was approaching and headed straight at me. With tales of local pirates I was alarmed. All I could do was start the auxiliary motor to avoid them and have flares ready. Or should I be passive and not resist?

Gradually it loomed larger; what kind of vessel was it?

I needn't have worried. It was a Chilean long-liner fishing boat. It simply swept past. I guess it was pure boredom or curiosity that had them come past to check us out. With a massive wave (of relief on my side) they were on their way. Radio contact was futile as we would not have understood each other.

Later that day I had a totally different kind of visitor. It was a massive cruise ship — the Island Princess — out of Bermuda. She is one of the largest in the world and I guessed had followed me by a few days around Cape Horn, being too large to go through Panama,

She went past and I thought that was that. But sometime later, while below deck, I looked up and saw it hovering over us in the evening light. A little shocked, I grabbed the hand-held VHF and called the ship on channel 16. I quickly established contact and explained that I was fine and would have called if I needed assistance.

Apparently some passengers had reported to the Bridge that they thought I might be in trouble.

They turned around. They seemed relaxed about it and went on their way.

So with that, in the comfort of fresh socks and as a tribute to the Souffle du Nord's collection of odd socks I finish with a selection of two expressions.

"Sock it to me, Sock it to me, Sock it to me......"

or

"Enda, you're a hard man... hard as socks...."

I was never sure if that was a compliment or an insult. Being positive as the voyage of our ship sails on, I opt for the former.

Δ Log, Day 31, Act III

We have been trapped for several days. To say I am frustrated and deflated is an understatement. It is so bad that an EGM of the South Atlantic Residents Association ended in apathy. As we enter our second month at sea there is talk of cannibalism, a Uruguayan world-famous school and rugby.

It's one extreme to another.

We have been locked, seemingly, in a never-ending high-pressure system. It was spread wide on either side and difficult to escape. Instead we are catching snippets of wind here, there and everywhere to slowly and painfully make our way up along the coast.

It's been a bit like the doldrums coming early on steroids.

But it's busy; there is lots to do though motivation on board is low.

When on track, on course in a breeze the world is the

greatest place to be. But at times like this you need all your staying power and mental strength to remain sane and focused.

I was also sick in my stomach. A mixture of canned tuna, blackcurrant juice, caramel coffee and potato did not help as it all came up again. Luckily we have plenty of supplies on board.

We are seeking to avoid the high pressure and are way out in the Atlantic as we slowly creep north. Argentina is ahead. It borders Uruguay where I first visited the capital Montevideo 25 years ago. Through a friend's introduction, it was a privilege to stay at the Stella Maris school with a group of Irish Christian Brothers. Their order established the school in 1955 and reported to Dublin.

With a large staff, the school was run by about eight brothers at the time — though I understand this has scaled back considerably with fewer and fewer vocations.

The school had more than 700 students and educated the country's elite. The school was to become world famous for bizarre reasons.

The order had come to Uruguay to bring the concept of Christianity back to society through education. It had been lost through successive dictatorships and bans on religion.

Stella Maris, named by the founder Brother Patrick Kelly, a devotee of the Virgin Mary, had become one of the best and most exclusive schools in the country.

This second smallest country in South America has a population of just more than 3.4m — half live in Montevideo. In 2013 it was named as the country of the year by the Economist magazine. Its laws are now liberal — from same-sex marriage to the legalisation of cannabis and it is one of the most socially developed countries in the region.

The Stella Maris school paved the way for Rugby Union

to be developed. In 1972 a school team and supporters were aboard an Uruguay airforce plane when it crashed in the Andes. After several days all hope was lost and the search was called off.

But a truly amazing story of survival was to unfurl.

After 72 days, only 16 of the 45 on board had survived. And they did so by eating their dead fellow travellers. It became the subject of a book (*ALIVE: The Story of the Andes' Survivors*) and a major film.

Δ Log, Day 35, Act III

Each day we slowly work our way up along the coast. The next goal is the Equator which is 2,000 miles away. Each day it gets warmer. The layers are coming off.

It's only when you count out each mile that you realise the scale of Brazil alone.

In the light airs, the South Atlantic Residents Association has also been active — discussing the currency against the US dollar and other affairs of the economy.

All fresh provisions are exhausted, as are the 'sweet things'.

All food supplies for members are monitored.

For body nourishment, it's now down to the basic Back Country dehydrated food to supply enough calories each day. This is supplemented by plenty of fresh water — made from the ocean by our magical de-salination plant on board — as well as my Revive Active dietary supplements.

It's a 24/7 or 25/8 constancy on the alert. Sailing through day and night blind, you simply never know what is going to happen next.

Long periods of inactivity are interspersed with intense bursts of being mad busy.

As with the Wizard of Oz it is the journey rather than getting there.

Given that there are virtually no weather systems, highs or lows in these settled conditions, it's hard to do anything clever to move the boat faster. While we are only racing against ourselves on the water — and others on computers — there is a strong competitive instinct that strives to get the best performance to do justice to the boat and team.

As a thoroughbred of the ocean you cannot half-sail her in the same way you cannot be half-pregnant.

Each day I marvel about how the IMOCA ocean sailing class design has developed and continues to evolve. And how one person can sail faster than a Volvo 65 which is bigger and has a crew of 10.

The daytime wind tends to be lighter. Our strategy is to stay on the tack closest to the layline rather than going to either corner of the course for better weather systems.

Each night the wind, with the thermal effect from the ocean and temperature difference, tends to increase to 10 to 15 knots. During the day 4 to 10 knots is the norm; an odd time it goes flat calm.

The constant challenge is to try to get the boat moving faster than the wind. In reality we create our own wind from movement that makes it happen. Given the right angle, sometimes I get her up to 9 knots in 6 or so knots of wind. This way, by always keeping moving, we can keep the average up and gradually, mile by mile, graft our way north. We are unlikely to make Le Sables d' Olonne for St Patrick's Day or my family reunion but it is as it is.

¶ ¶ ¶ ¶

The mind wanders.

Our South Atlantic Residents Association is wealthy. Our money supply is infinite and beats Bitcoin all the time. As a matter of fiction, a wealthy American came to stay at our luxury accommodation. He deposited $1,000 for the en-suite room forward and, being early in the day, went for a long walk on deck. I took the money and paid our fish supplier $1,000. This fisherman in turn owed his boat builder $1,000 and he was paid. The same boat builder owed me $1,000 for services and kindly paid me back.

It all happened quite quickly. But didn't the American return and announce he would not stay. And since he had not checked in to the cabin, he demanded his money back. Which he got. Therefore everyone was paid and nobody was out of pocket. This begs the question (which has been racking the brains of the Residents Association): what is money?

Historically it was based on a finite commodity such as gold and not just fresh air.

On a much bigger scale, Donal Trump looks set to increase, instead of reducing, the massive US deficits.

So like his huge property bankruptcy history, based on debt, he is doing the same to the US. Some day when we least expect it, the penny will drop and all the money the US Fed are making out of fresh air will have no value. Based on nothing, the economy will collapse while the US, being the US, will reinvent itself with a lot of pain for us all.

So the world is in for a shock.

The Ice Age did not happen over hundreds of years. It came quickly. Water gets cold and at a certain instant it freezes.

Likewise water gets hot and at a certain instant it boils. Each situation brings massive change to the water. One, hard ice. One, steam.

And now there is little difference between our unit of currency as fresh air here on the south Atlantic and the

US money — based on nothing. I think a big storm will come and we'll all be in trouble. So prepare and batten down the hatches.

Δ Log 38, Act III

Some 150 miles off Rio de Janeiro we inadvertently sailed into the middle of one of the largest offshore oilfields in the world. Between drilling platforms and supporting vessels it is enormous. And it was risky, picking our way through. This was the highlight of the past few days during which I dipped to a new low.

For a time, with the carnival just over, Rio was a real possibility as we came within 80 miles of it before going back east again out sea.

In reality all the boat problems and my psychological issues were looking for solutions. And we are finding them as we creep along. And will continue to do so.

Winds have almost been non-existent as we go from cloud to cloud. Power had become a problem. This is critical: from Nav, to self-steering, safety lights and making enough water. With the auxiliary engine and charger out of action, we did not have enough speed to power the hydro-generator.

Making things worse, the temperature was 30°C with no protection from the sun to the south west, as we sail north east at the height of summer. I was cooking and could have been eaten rare.

¶ ¶ ¶ ¶

First I thought it was another sailboat, given the unusual vertical shape of the large oil rig. Then it kept getting bigger and bigger. Then, as darkness fell and as gas was being burned off, the massive flames from the other rig made it seem like Christmas. We found it to be the Lula oilfield on the Santos Basin, considered to be the Western Hemisphere's largest discovery of oil in the last 30 years. Upper estimates put it at 30 billion barrels. And not so long ago we were being told our planet was running out of oil.

Discovered in 2008 by Petrobas, the Brazilian state oil conglomerate, the first oil delivery was made in 2011. The fields are targeted to reach 500,000 barrels a day.

The oil is located in water about two miles deep and then another three miles through salt, sand and rocks. It works because of huge advances in oil-extraction technology.

The attractions for the big oil companies are that resource nationalism denies them access to three-quarters of the world's known reserves. The economics and politics offshore are simpler. Out here they only have to contend with obscure organisations such as our South Atlantic Residents Association. There is nobody else to object for thousands of miles in this vast open space.

Considering the complexity of the geological formations deep down, there is a lot of risk. Development does not come cheap. They spent $1bn before extracting anything while the ultimate costs of getting all the oil out is put at between $50bn and $100bn.

Developing this massive reserve was not without controversy. As part of getting started, there were several accidents, massive explosions and deaths.

And what was said to be one of the largest rigs in the world sank.

¶ ¶ ¶ ¶

Back on board our little ship, I was on high alert navigating through the oilfields. Strictly speaking I should not have been there, but to sail around them would have been a big diversion in the light airs. To conserve power, everything from the sat phone to the electronic barometer had to be turned off. And for several hours I hand-steered, which saved on the big power consumption of the self-steering system.

One day at a time.

Each day the Equator gets closer and closer. A remarkable contrast to our last big turning point, Cape Horn.

Crossing will be a milestone as, after we had passed through on the way out, my grand-daughter Feile was born.

As they say:

'When the going gets tough, the tough get going
And the big secret to good navigation
Is to steer around the rocks
Power be damned.'

Δ Log, Day 40, Act III

Last night we got to within 20 miles of Vitoria, a small city by Brazilian standards with a population of 350,000. Always an indicator of being close to land were the insects fatally attracted to the glow of my computer screen. I killed them. It reminds me why being away on the ocean is so attractive. No bugs, no infections, bacteria or, in my case, allergies. In other words, it's healthy.

So on this 40th day at sea I will update on my diet — the other part of being healthy. The third pillar is physical activity and here our skipper is demanding. There is no shortage of grinding and pulling ropes on this ship. I have rarely worked as physically hard in my life to date.

As a matter of fact I could be at risk of dying from health. It is also important to note that your skipper is distress-

A year later back in New Zealand South Island close to Queenstown, on a break before departing with my son Cormac prospecting for gold. We actually found a little and Cormac was following in the tradition of his great-great-grandfather who found gold in California and returned to Ireland with enough to afford a pub, wife and family (we're not sure which came first!) while at a relatively ancient age.

Kindly organised by Billy Walshe, a great help and friend in Auckland. A Maori Chief, Warahi Paki, blessed our boat prior to departing in a wonderful ceremony. Effectively celebrating New Zealand taking me in, helping rebuild, and sending me away for a safe passage celebrating the Sky, Earth and Ocean...

Prior to departing to finish the voyage, Maxime Buoy and Pierre-Antoine Tesson, who did an incredible job in getting ready, with Saoirse, Cormac and our mascot, 'Monkey On My Back'.

Above and right: Preparing to depart off Auckland.

Alone at sea again with my Spirit of Adventure Trust Kiwi gift, Paddy the Leprechaun and the Monkey on my Back — complete with the Maori good luck necklace...

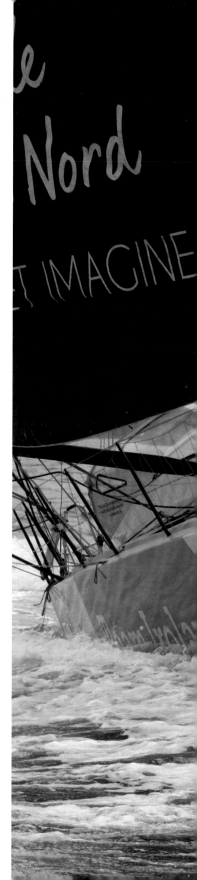

At sea again with a special sticker from College Sacre-Coeur in Dunkirk, incredible supporters led by Christophe Thilliez, their inspirational teacher.

A self-portrait complete with mascots Paddy the Leprechaun and Monkey on My Back, on rounding Cape Horn, February 16th, 2018, which was a wild and incredible moment.

The RIYC Flag Rounding Cape Horn, outlined in the background. It was a magic moment and the experience was everything and more, almost religious...

The Cruise Liner in close quarters which (kindly!) tried to rescue me, when I did not need to be rescued, after rounding Cape Horn. It was embarrassing!

It was a long slow slog up the South Atlantic from Cape Horn to the Equator. Unexpectedly, not charted, I ran into massive oil fields some 150 miles offshore from Brazil.

This time President Higgins kindly got through on the sat phone, exactly as we crossed the Equator, and I was dressed in my pirate captain's outfit for the occasion — a celebration.

Left and below:
approaching the
finishing line.

That incredible moment, 510 days after setting out, I'm back to where we started. After crossing the 'unofficial finish line' off Les Sables d'Olonne, I've travelled around the world solo with one stop — and a long one at that — sailing around New Zealand.

While a very personal quest, the circumnavigation fired imaginations in France and it was flattering that several thousand came out to greet us home.

After months alone, the adjustment for human immersion was instant. The media and attention was surreal. Notice in the crowd (below) the "Enda Masks" and Sean Lemass, with others who were also there at the start.

Ahoy! The crowd at Les Sables d'Olonne.

The barber at Charles de Gaulle recognised the sailor and gave him a free beard trim en route and a wee drop of whiskey to celebrate getting back to Ireland. Ironically our island nation gave an incredible welcome on the previous return home from New Zealand celebrating the loss of my mast. Failing conveyed hero status. However, actually completing the circumnavigation did not rate at home — which is entirely appropriate. I liked that and it keeps us humble. And, with the wonderful exception of President Higgins, it proves, conclusively, that failure often rates higher than success...

Subsequent to competing the circumnavigation we got a great welcome back to Monaco by Prince Albert, Patron of the Vendée Globe Race. His Irish pub in the Palace now has a bottle of whiskey which has been around the world — and Paddy the Leprechaun also has a new home!

To finish, I donned a shirt and tie to present at an Irish Breakfast at Yacht Club Monaco. Colette Twomey supplied the Clonakilty black pudding and rashers, while Brigitta Hess provided the Burren smoked salmon. And our band from the Vendée start, led by Cormac, played "Whiskey in the Castle" to the tune of "Whiskey in the Jar" sung by Peadar Gill.

The somewhat bemused Albert's Palace was an appropriate backdrop. We also raised funds for the Atlantic Youth Trust Charity.

Co-skippered by Joan Mulloy and Thomas Ruyant, our boat had an impressive 4th in the IMOCA Globe Series hosted by YCM. In my view it is the best such club in the world — superbly run by CEO Bernard d'Alessandri with great team members such as Charlotte Mille. It was a very appropriate "end", with an "a" added, for this author's global ocean adventures — and a great launchpad for Joan, a talented adventurer and sailor.

The boat is pictured below off Monaco and, right, at the presentation with Albert, whose mother Grace Kelly's family is from Mayo, birthplace of Grace O'Malley — from whom Joan is descended — and who will hopefully go around the world, with our support, next time (without stopping!).

Other than scale, sailing my IMOCA 60 above 30 knots surfing down massive Southern Ocean waves is similar in some ways to sailing my SB20 dinghy "Bád KILCULLEN". She is pictured (left) with Jimmy and Jerry Dowling, for inclusion as the final pic as this book goes to the printers, by special request to Jerry — and dedicated to our SB20 fleet and to boast without shame to have been race winners in a blustery, shifty day on Dublin Bay, August 22nd, 2019.

With President Michael D. Higgins at Áras an Úachtaráin, celebrating the circumnavigation and discussing The Atlantic Youth Trust "briefing" for the tall ship 'Grace O'Malley'. Left to right: Anne Chambers, Brian Fallon, Sarah Murphy, Saoirse O'Coineen, Enda O'Coineen, President Michael D. Higgins, Roisin O'Coineen, Roger Courtney, Tina McKenzie, John Toner, John Killeen, Daniela Liebing and Brian Lynch.

ingly sane while the rest of the world, as we all know, is crazy.

Tempting as it was to land at Vitoria, the Residents Association voted against. When Googled, the fact the local police have been on strike, murders are on the rise and people are protesting about crime, all helped to swing the decision. So we headed straight back offshore and away again from so-called civilisation.

¶ ¶ ¶ ¶

Last night off Vitoria was nerve wracking. Between all the oil rigs, service vessels and fishing boats and being without AIS an extra demanding watch was warranted. To stay alert, every 30 minutes or so, I set the alarm.

Brazil and its enormous coastline seem to go on forever. As do the oil rigs. Our target and magical turning point is at Recife on the north east corner. From there we plan to veer to port, picking up the bottom end of the north east and easterly trade winds, then blast our way to the Equator and home.

Not being aware of the wells and rigs made it feel like we found oil all on our own. Except that Joan Mulloy of Team Ireland Ocean Racing reported to our skipper that she knew all about them. She had toiled as a sub-contractor doing computer analysis designing pipelines running between drillship and seabed — which she never saw. Yes, it was all from an industrial estate in Galway's Ballybrit for the Brazilian conglomerate Petrobras.

Joan, by the way, has an aspiration to do the Vendée; she has the talent and ability. She deserves our support. This year she is campaigning a Figaro in France based in Lorient with a regatta in Les Sables d'Olonne over St Patrick's weekend where I plan to unofficially finish the Vendée.

¶ ¶ ¶ ¶

A regular staple diet on board is a challenge after 40 days at sea, so it's down to basics now. All the fresh food and sweet things are long gone.

On the food preparation front . . . while in New Zealand I took a trip to Invercargill at the bottom of the south island where there is an Irish pub — and Back Country cuisine.

The great pub is called Waxie and its professional manager is Hamish Baird. Oddly, it is owned by a local government trust. It has joined the Irish Pubs global network.

Back Country make uniquely convenient food dishes, designed specially for outdoor adventurers. After I heard about it I thought it important to see the products at first hand. Following a tour of the factory I went through the menu and ordered three months' supply.

So meal preparation is ultra simple. I power boil just enough water, slice open the foil packet, mix it up, allow it to sit for 10 minutes and that's it.

The technology is interesting: massive ovens extract all the moisture from the ingredients, and when you restore the moisture returns you have a perfect meal.

And while all food suppliers must have a use-by-dates, in theory these meals can last forever if kept perfectly sealed. I wager that had Back Country food been available for Irishman Ernest Shackelton's visits to Antarctica, he would have had a supply. In addition to finding some perfectly preserved bottles of whiskey under his Antarctic cabin, they might well have found a Back Country supply ready to eat.

The only other staple in my diet is a sachet of porridge every morning. And a meal of Revive Active ingredients by a Galway company that produces a range of natural food supplements. I highly recommend them. Even when not on the ocean, I supplement my diet with their products.

Mind you, my culinary skills and dietary demands are minimalist. Like an ability to roll up and sleep anywhere, my stomach is resilient.

So much so that in a fit of understandable anger a while back my wife fed me pet food without telling me.

It was pre-mobile phone days and there was a waiting list for lines. It was more like a dream list for our new box-starter home in suburban Dublin. Instead of going straight home for dinner one evening after work, I met an old friend Derek, for a pint of plain or two — and left my new bride at home waiting.

As can happen after a few pints, I invited Derek home for dinner. Little did I realise that my commander-in-chief was waiting diligently with a romantic meal for two.

When I got home (all smiles, God bless her), she fed Derek my dinner, had hers and I got the pet food in the middle of the rice.

You could have cut the tension in the air with a knife. In a vain attempt to make up, I quickly finished dinner and dug an even larger grave for myself by complimenting her on the meal. I even asked for more. She kept the identity of my meal a secret until Derek had gone.

¶ ¶ ¶ ¶

Fortunately the Resident's Association has a no-pet policy, excluding, of course, Adolf our monkey, Paddy our Leprechaun and our little bear. So as we sail into the dark night and to conclude today's log about diet, oil rigs and having a pint after work, I quote from Flann O'Brien:

'When money's tight and hard to get
and your horse has also ran
When all you have is a heap of debt
A PINT OF PLAIN IS YOUR ONLY MAN.'

Δ Log, Day 45, Act III

Gradually, and painfully, we are beating north and upwind in a choppy rolling sea. With 20 knot winds, we are inching closer to top right corner of Brazil. My worry is that the sail repairs will hold up. Ironically, had we been some days earlier, or some days later, the winds would have been more in our favour.

Could the poor luck in the wind's direction be down to my Maori Pounmu good luck stone around my neck being broken? It happened when I was grinding the winches. Hopefully the bad luck will be temporary (I have replaced it with the spare) as I was also blessed by the Maori priest in Auckland; and it is a lighter, sleeker Pounmu stone.

On reaching Recife and turning the corner, the winds should come our way. And from here our Mecca: the Equator. I have little doubt it is filled with vestal virgins and comely maidens dancing at the Meridian with King Neptune.

After that, it's the trade winds; up past the Caribbean and doldrums, west around the Azores High and a brisk spring arrival in Le Sables d'Olonne, eastern France. We hope.

And I remain nervous.

To make progress the Residents Association has been active. With each tack and wind shift, our navigation tactics are debated. But the exasperating experience in the hot sun has convinced me that democracy does not work. And during all this debate an old friend, John McDonald, called from the middle of the Cook Straits on his way to Sydney. He says he has been following our logs and the "skipper's slow demise into insanity".

The Cook Straits are so named after the great explorer whose 250th anniversary is being celebrated shortly in New Zealand. The straits separate the north Island from the south Island.

Decision-making is difficult in a democracy. It's divisive, inefficient, slow and makes it difficult to get things done. As Adolf Hitler might say (as declared by our resident monkey and Association President — also named Adolf): "Either lead, follow or get out of the way."

Be that as it may, democracy has been the best system for the human race to date. However, at some point you have to make a decision, tack on the wind-shifts, change course and get on with it.

On John Mc's comment about madness: Throughout my life and its various adventures, whether it's starting a business, heading out on my own across the Atlantic in a 16 foot inflatable experimental sailing life raft or meeting Jackie Onassis, people say: "Sure he's mad, odd as two left feet and not all there." Or something to that effect.

This implies you are a person to be wary of; to put down; to avoid his ideas, ways of thinking and not to accept. In short we fear agents of change.

I believe labelling something as 'mad' to be a cop-out. It basically shows the person making the comment does not understand. And when that happens, people are quick to put what you are doing outside their comprehension zone.

By going out on a limb you are breaking with convention. This makes many people feel uncomfortable and threatened. You become a subconscious threat to their norm; and for that reason they box you out.

But to undertake unusual activities, such as taking a 60ft-boat, on your own around the world, you have to be distressingly sane. Quite simply a person who is 'mad' in the conventional sense would not survive. The reality is you have to be seriously organised to prepare for voyages and run a boat, and make a business work: "Unless chaos is organised it is panic." So my message from this log to all is: Relax. Don't worry Sure we'll all be a long time dead and only the good people die young, anyway.

Now after saying all that, each minute, hour and day, I live on the edge and take risks.

Our boat is constantly powering along, but such are the forces and loads at play you never know what is going to happen next. Walking the decks, changing sails, tacking or gybing — anything can happen.

Just yesterday after emptying a bucket of waste (the biodegradable variety — need I say more?) I slipped and fell after mistiming a wave with the bucket in the other hand. My leg was hurt. The end of a winch handle narrowly escaped poking my eye out.

Living here in total isolation, I could be in a space capsule or trapped in a prison cell. Here off the coast of Brazil, as one does, I re-read some 30 verses from Oscar Wilde's famous 'Ballad of Reading Gaol'.

That was his last work after being sent to prison for being gay. On release, he suffered ill-health and lived in a low-rent Paris hotel. He is said to have hated his bedroom wallpaper so much that his last words were: "Something has to go."

The same could be said for this capsule where I have been boxed this past 45 days. "The wind has to shift."

Wilde in the Ballad was referring to love. He wrote about a friend whom he had met in prison (jailed for killing his wife) who was destined for the gallows.

From my cell on this boat, where the headwinds have killed my love of sailing (for the moment) I extract and co-relate meaning while not ultimately agreeing with the great writer's thesis.

And while I would never kill a wife, with justification the wife could kill me. Go figure.

'Yet each man kills the things he loves
By each let this be heard
Some do it with a bitter look
Some with a flattering word
The coward does it with a kiss
The brave man with a sword.
Some kill their love when they are young
And some when they are old
Some strangle with the hands of Lust
Some with the hands of Gold.
The kindest use a knife
Because the dead soon grow cold
'Some love too little, some too long
Some sell, and others buy.'

LESSONS FROM CHAPTER 17
↗ It is the journey rather than getting there.
↗ Luck — really, you make your own luck.

Crossing the Equator had been a truly magical moment. It was early Friday, 16th March after 48 days at sea. King Neptune and his court gave us a personal audience and a warm welcome. Evidently he had remembered us from the outward journey. Then President Higgins came on the line and congratulated us on completing the circumnavigation.

Chapter 18
The President Calls

THE President of Ireland's office called on the sat phone. Without thinking I answered: "South Atlantic Residents Association. How may I direct your call?"

Confused, the other person almost hung up. He must have thought he'd got a wrong number. Petrified that we might have a repeat of last time at Christmas off Tasmania, when President Higgins failed to get through, I shouted: "No really, it's me."

I got him back in time and clarified my mistake. The call had also been an hour earlier than expected. That said, the timing could not have been better. I guess his office was tracking us on the satellite.

¶ ¶ ¶ ¶

Crossing the Equator had been a truly magical moment. It was early Friday 16th March after 48 days at sea. King Neptune and his court gave us a personal audience and a warm welcome. Evidently he had remembered us from the outward journey. Then President Higgins came on the line and congratulated us on completing the circumnavigation.

This was indeed a great honour not just for me, but for all our partners, friends and those who supported the project.

We talked for 10 minutes on a range of subjects — from the success of his recent visit to New Zealand to celebrating St Patrick's Day. We discussed it being the national day in Monserrat in the Caribbean (which I now leave to port).

I dressed in my 18th century pirate captain's uniform for the president and to meet King Neptune. It was not visible on the phone; only to the lone skipper but who cares? The original idea was to wear the uniform rounding Cape Horn. However, it was no time for play-acting in the ferocious wind and waves.

Since then I've had more excuses to wear it as I was nominated an East Coast Table Captain for the Frères de la Côte (the brotherhood of the coast). This organisation, in various guises, goes back more than 200 years when ships' captains and owners, originating in the Caribbean, would meet. They would feast and share information on friend and foe. The gathering was called a Boucan — hence the term Buccaneers. Now there are autonomous tables all around the world, each different, but guided by the core principles of common brotherhood and love of the sea. Many years ago they decided not to open a bank account since it would be too easy to trace.

¶ ¶ ¶ ¶

After the president and the Equator, we were headed east towards the western Caribbean and Windward islands. We left them to port with the prevailing north easterlies. And as we moved north we veered east and south-east to bring us up towards the Azores to pick up the north easterlies to the left of the Azores High to take us on the last leg home.

¶ ¶ ¶ ¶

The founding frère, Boucan, was on the island of Tortuga close to Haiti. The last time I'd been in Haiti — we landed one Monday morning — I was greeted with my first task: to get our then manager out of gaol.

She was running the Irish Village and Irish Embassy pub. With a population of around 10 million, Haiti is one of the poorest countries in the world. So you might ask, rightly, why an Irish pub?

Well it happened like this.

Together with a business partner, Conchur de Barra, we had formed the business in Haiti. It was a mad and wild move and ranks as the craziest enterprise I have undertaken. Conchur, a good friend, is from Fermoy and now floats somewhere between Prague and Brussels running an assortment of pubs.

The idea came from a plea to businessmen, and a real desire to help Haiti, led by Denis O'Brien and a group of entrepreneurs including Leslie Buckley, through the Haven and Soul of Haiti Charities. Denis has made a big success of his phone business there and in turn contributed a lot, believing corporates should put profit back into the community.

In addition to being good for society, it's good for business.

After the earthquake some years back the country was in a mess. They needed help and, rather than make a charitable donation, which in retrospect might have been smarter in our case, we decided to set up the Irish Village.

It did some good and helped the country in a way. The idea was to create employment and training in the hospitality sector as a basis for tourism and self-help.

With the destruction of all the normal social networks in Haiti, the pub was a place for aid workers to meet, relax and share information. Quite often informal contacts like that bring co-operation.

¶ ¶ ¶ ¶

When I went to Prague for the first time, Frank Haughton who had been there a short time had opened the James Joyce pub. It was just after the communists left. And it was at the pub I met the lawyers, financiers, government advisers and so forth with whom I quickly made connections. We shared war stories and I got to know the market.

Haiti desperately lacked places for such social interaction.

It started out as a pub project but became a much larger concept — a village. We leased a school compound which had broken up in the earthquake. More than a million dollars later, we ended up with several retail shops, offices, a rooftop restaurant and the Irish embassy. Such was its novelty that at one time we had a kitchen worker whom the police suspected of a crime. But they were afraid to enter the pub to arrest the suspect because they thought it was a real embassy.

It was successful, initially, with foreign staff running the business, employing more than 100. It was complete with a marble counter, elaborate woodwork and old church furniture shipped from Ireland. Our idea was to generate a social enterprise where money would be reinvested to grow and train Haitians and to build a service culture.

Gradually, to make it more economical, we reduced the number of expats. In truth they could only last a while; Haiti was a really tough place to work. Conditions were primitive, it was corrupt, and there were shootings. With very little work ethic, getting things done was a nightmare.

Anyway, one night our bar manager and her boyfriend got drunk on a day off at the local Caribe Hotel complex. They had a big row. She stormed off and crashed our 4x4 jeep. On returning to the complex both she and her boyfriend were arrested and put in jail. That was the Sunday night.

Her boyfriend's father, skilled in how things operated locally, quickly got his son out. But he left her behind; she was not popular and had rowed with the police when handcuffed.

So the Monday morning, immediately after landing from Miami for a few days to review progress, I was told the local police wanted $80,000 to let her out. And since I was the owner on-site, I was asked what I was going to do about it.

As foreigners, we were soft targets. They were trying it on. The big risk was that, as a foreigner too, she would have ended up down-country in the horrible women's prison waiting six months or more for trial. Not getting her out could be akin to a death sentence. As her employer, it was our responsibility to act.

We were subsequently told we could get it down to $5,000.

Then it took clever work by our German-French-Haitian lawyer, who made a claim that as a result of injuries our manager needed medical care. That got her to the hospital where she knew the matron. The police conceded and moved her to hospital. But they posted an armed guard outside her door to keep their ransom secure.

While she only had a wrist injury from the handcuffs, the matron had her entire arm and shoulder made up in a great, big plaster cast. She also hooked her up with an intravenous drip feed. She was then photographed in her hospital bed. The picture, up on Facebook with claims of police brutality, went viral. The story quickly reached police command. I think it possibly even got to the minister. There was too much heat. Not long afterwards, the local branch got the order to release her. We paid nothing.

Two days later our manager was on a plane back to Brussels, never to return.

That is just one of many crazy examples of running an enterprise in Haiti. The final straw, as the business became more challenged with local management, was when one of our doormen was shot dead in a territorial fight between two security companies. I was back in Ireland when the news came. Not long afterwards we closed.

¶ ¶ ¶ ¶

Meanwhile back at sea and sailing south west of Haiti, the kamikaze fish struck again. It was shortly after the president's congratulatory phone call on completing the circumnavigation. We were also followed by a tropical squall of 30 knot winds as we entered home waters with only 3,000 miles to go. Here's the log:

Δ Log, Day 52, Act III

The squall left us struggling for control as we approached the edge of the doldrums on the way in. But the blast of tropical wind moved on as quickly as it came, while the flying fish persisted in attacking. When they hit the decks, I though it was gunfire. Like pellets from a shotgun blast, they jumped through the waves, expecting something different, and got a rude shock when they landed on our ocean real-estate. Drowning on our decks they stayed to be cooked alive and die in the morning sun.

Since then, we have negotiated our way out of the doldrums, which lasted for only about 100 miles. Likewise, these flying fish are a sure sign you are getting into the trade winds. We are heading north-west in a steady 20 knots leaving the Caribbean to port and the Cape Verde islands to starboard.

¶ ¶ ¶ ¶

Our direction is way off course from where we want to go. However, as we move north west, the trades gradually veer to the east allowing us to track around to the north. And then, not going further east than 40 degrees and from 30 north we will hit the west side of the Azores High.

Then we pick up the prevailing westerlies to take us to the finish at Le Sables d'Olonne. I hope it is before Easter in time for some chocolate and eggs. We are now down to water, dehydrated foods and food supplements. Food is scarce.

¶ ¶ ¶ ¶

It has been like entering a different planet since rounding the corner at Recife on the north east corner of Brazil. One was hot headwinds and slow progress. The other has been cooling trade winds, off-wind sailing and the magic of crossing the Equator.

Meanwhile it's champagne sailing on the edge of the beautiful Caribbean Ocean. We have steady cooling trade winds as we make progress directly north. Days like this make the pain on other days bearable and it all worthwhile. Great to be alive. Sometimes we want the voyage to go on forever and other times there is an urgency to get off and resume shore life.

One complication is the amount of surface-floating seaweed. It keeps snarling our hydro-generator which charges the batteries. Between the self-steering, computer system, night navigation lights and water de-salination, power supply is vital. I have to watch this and constantly clear the weed.

While I am sailing conservatively, I do want to get home in time for Easter. So the boat is well powered up and I have 3,000 litres of water. That is about 6,400 lbs in weight on the side to keep the boat balanced. This is the same as having more than 30, 100-kilo men each on the weather-rail.

The boat has 12 water ballast tanks in all; six either side. They are configured for either going up-wind, down-wind or reaching, or some combination in between. As you can imagine, filling and managing these tanks is a complex task in itself. That work alone — transferring water from one side to the other in a tack — takes about 20 minutes with a lot of pipe opening and closing and suction.

Δ Log, Day 60 at Sea, Act III

My Dubarry, Galway boots were squeezed on. These boots

were made for sailing and nowadays are sailing all over the world.

Meanwhile progress is brilliant. We power sail north east, driven by a 27 to 34 knot southerly — almost gale force — on the western side of the Azores High.

We are surfing the waves, with up to 24 knots boat speed. I am keen to finish — Easter eggs beckon — while all the time I remain on edge. Like eggs: fragile.

I put on my Galway boots for the first time in five weeks as I reapply the layers of protection each day moving north. It's bad and good. Bad, because it's getting colder, wetter and the seas are more intense. Good, because after clearing the Azores, it's the final 1,200-mile sprint home and the fulfilment of a goal, dream and mission.

The fascinating Azores Atlantic islands are the next big turning point. My mind escapes as I get into reading Greek philosophers. Sure what else would you be doing when things are going well?

The Azores stand out as massive islands. That is, if you look at all the ancient maps of the world and the Atlantic Ocean. Essentially the map-makers and ships captains, on whom they relied, exaggerated their size. They are really just small dots on a world map. This larger-than-real representation reflected their importance as meeting points, centres for trade, commerce, navigation, provisioning, repairs etc.

Strategically located, the population of some 250,000 is a mixture of several nationalities. With seven islands in total, each with a varying climate and personality, they are one of two independent states within Portugal.

This time I shall not be stopping. However, it's good to have them near should repairs be needed. My last visit to St Miguel (several years ago) was after sailing through the tail end of a hurricane on a voyage from Florida. I was in bits, but quickly recovered. I'll never forget the rejuvenating bliss, on a tired body, of the incredible volcanic natural hot water spas.

¶ ¶ ¶ ¶

The Azores, as landmarks, reflect the essence of achievement by goal setting — in much the same way the Equator and Cape Horn ranked on this voyage. It's a way I survive. While it takes 200 hard grinds to furl the J2 headsail, I set a goal of 50 at a time. Aristotle described goal setting — conscious and sub-conscious — as the essence of life itself.

He called it the teleology of purpose. Perhaps as a result of his preoccupation with biological studies, the philosopher was impressed by the idea that both animate and inanimate behaviour is directed towards some final purpose (telos) or goal.

Aristotle maintained it was common to explain the behaviour of humans, institutions and nations in terms of purpose and goals. Even sub-consciously as humans our goal is to survive. Then a higher level consciously sets goals as individuals and communities become drivers of society. Otherwise it would be like being on the ocean going nowhere, drifting aimlessly. Teleology brings us to a higher level.

On this boat for me, or in the wizard of Oz, it's the journey, not actually getting there that gives the adventure and buzz.

For that reason I will not be sure what to do when we finish in Les Sables d'Olonne — other than the goal of physical pleasures such as making love, eating some juicy steaks, enjoying a big Easter egg and a good party with friends.

The other great philosopher I have been reading is Thales of Miletus. He preceded Aristotle and is said to be the first natural scientist and analytical philosopher in western intellectual history. For him the entire basis of the world as we know it is water. Yes, water.

The first principle of life is vapour by evaporation and solid by freezing. It's the essence of everything and two-thirds of the world, at least, is covered by it. All life is supported by moisture and he postulated that water was the single causal principle behind the natural world. Without it, there is no life.

Mind you, he was a little off the mark when he reckoned the earth was flat and floated on water much like a log or a ship. He even accounted for earthquakes as being due to waves rocking the earth. Can you imagine the life of an ancient ship's captain sailing across oceans — not sure when he would reach the edge and fall off!

Thales was the first to give naturalistic explanation to the universe. His logic about water was central to this. He also concluded that the mind of the world was God in all things — a fundamental for religions as they evolved. So between Thales and Aristotle defining society by goals, targets and water being the catalyst, perhaps we have it all figured out on this voyage?

Anyway, my last word in today's log must be with Socrates (470 BC): 'The only thing I know is that I know nothing.'

LESSONS FROM CHAPTER 18
- ↗ Water is indeed central to the universe
- ↗ When you're feeling down, you're one thought away from changing how you feel.

Chapter 19
Stormy Finish
And Landfall

IT was dark. There was a storm raging as I gradually worked north past the Azores and was about 100 miles off Cape Finisterre. Only 350 miles. So close and yet so far.

It had become quite cold moving into the Bay of Biscay in March. Lying in my navigation chair, I was alarmed to see the wind move north of 40 knots in a vicious squall. It was time to shorten sail and furl the jib. I put my foot, destined for my seaboots, on the floor and instead stood in water. I swore. Whatever else, keeping socks dry and warm was mission critical.

I thought I'd left the hatch open. But no; instead there were tonnes of water sloshing around the bilges. I was scared. So close and yet so far. My mind raced. Were we in danger of sinking? How fast was it filling? Should I run for the coast?

Then the boat heeled more. I struggled to get on my boots, even if wet, and my oilskins. Whatever the problem, in these cold conditions, it is vital to stay protected from the elements. No sooner had I surfaced on deck when there was a crash gybe. The wind and enormous waves were too much for the self-steering in a turbulent ocean. The boat lay on its side, main stuck against the runner with the keel angled the wrong way. And the wind howled.

After some struggle I eventually got the boat back under control and on course.

But where was the water coming from? Was this the end?

The boat was still filling. I simply could not understand it. There was no time; nor could I afford the luxury of panicking. I quickly inspected the hull and deduced it was on the starboard side. So I went back up on deck and gybed immediately, headed for the Spanish coastline.

This lifted the starboard side clear of the water where I suspected the leak to be. I explored the option to make a dart for shore.

Believe me, there is no more efficient way to bail water than a frightened man with a bucket. Around 40 minutes later the bulk of it was out and the leak — being on the other tack — had stopped for the moment. Eventually I found it was the valve for filling the water ballast tanks that had been sucked open. Fortunately it was only bent slightly and I managed to get it shut and sealed. With another gybe I was back on course.

It was just one of many dramas on this racing machine. Every day I am on the edge; you never know what problems will confront you next.

Δ Log, Day 66, Act III

Appropriately this day, the feast of the Resurrection, Easter Sunday April 1st is the last log of SDN Kilcullen.

From the lowest of lows on losing my mast half way around, I feel I have come back from the dead.

I briefly turned off the satellite tracker and sent an email that I would finish at the Aran Islands instead. It was an April fool's joke which never worked.

It is not just 66 days alone at sea since New Zealand but since January 1st 2015 when we decided to go for it. And after experiencing the full range of personal emotions, physical challenge, fear and jubilation I have been on edge right to the finish line.

The voyage has been a bit like a passage through life. But now I am weary, keen to finish my Journey to the Edge. I take words from John Boyle O'Reilly's 'Passage' (and when he uses the term 'man' he must mean in this generality both sexes).

'The world was made when a man was born.
He must taste for himself the forbidden springs.
He can never take warning from old fashioned things
He must fight as a boy, he must drink as a youth
He must kiss, he must love, he must swear to the truth.
And so he goes on until the world grows old.
Till his tongue has grown cautious, his heart has grown cold.
Till the smile leaves his mouth, and the ring leaves his laugh
He grows formal with men and with women polite,
And distrustful of both when they're out of sight.
Then he eats for his palate, and drinks for his head
And loves for his pleasure, — and, 'tis time he was dead!'

Now I am really ready to sign that document, discussed earlier, that will allow family and friends to lock me up and throw away the key should I try at my age a repeat performance.

¶ ¶ ¶ ¶

Slowly in the distance, the French coast loomed larger. Landfalls after being on the ocean are always special. This was incredible — but I had to keep my nerve. Right to the end. Until I crossed that finish-line of Les Sables, anything could happen. Even though it was an unofficial finish I had to do it all on my own.

First tiny specks, then a little flotilla of small ribs in the choppy cold Atlantic grew bigger. Friends and family who had travelled over for my arrival were waving. It was truly amazing, one of those emotional high points that make all the other lows-of-lowest worthwhile. Again I had to pinch myself: Was this really happening?

The flotilla accompanied me for that last mile.

And yet I wanted it to continue.

In a bizarre way totally on my own, in this little world, for a moment I felt I did not want to leave it and go back to the other world.

I crossed the line like an emotional time bomb,

Then it was over.

A gang jumped on board and took control.

Thousands lined the famous Les Sables pier-head (the journey's finish in this town linked by umbilical cord to ocean and adventure) and embraced me. The mayor hosted a party and presented me with a medal, a sort of Freedom of the City. It was all a haze; so many well-wishers. I felt so privileged to have been able to undertake such an adventure.

The Irish homecoming

This time coming back to Ireland there was no party, no press, TV or radio interview calls. The first time, after suffering great failure, I had an incredible welcome home. But now virtually nothing.

And that is as it should be. I was more than happy to come home quietly and get on with the rest of my life. A new beginning.

The lesson for me was: if you want attention, put yourself out there in a public way and then fail. That is a good trajectory. As human beings, and in particular in Ireland, we sometimes take pleasure in other people's failures. Happily, that is changing but when it comes to news, 'disaster sells'. That is human nature the world over, not just on our little island. However, in Ireland our begrudgery is special. Essentially, if someone is doing well, by deduction, it is at the expense of someone else as opportunities are limited.

In the bigger world, such as the US, there are so many resources that everyone can do well. So you don't have to drag the successful person down because there is enough out there to make you successful as well.

Ultimately though, what you do and achieve is what matters. Newspapers, TV and being viral are short-lived. It's like a one-night stand. Have fun, make the best of it but there is no substance. A book like this, on the other hand (if it's good enough of course), is like getting married and can, hopefully, stand the test of time.

I was so lucky to be in a position to undertake such an adventure. To fulfil a life-long dream like this, at my stage in life, gives tremendous personal inner satisfaction to do it (relatively) quietly. It's almost a sort of smugness. The bottom line is we are all different. That is the wonder and the marvel of society, life and civilisation as we have come to know them. We are always striving, always at it — whatever it may be. Otherwise we're dead.

Next up is the start of the rest of my life. And the future starts now with something radically different — buying a national newspaper.

LESSONS FROM CHAPTER 19

↗ Whatever else, keeping dry feet is mission critical so always check that your boots are dry before putting your foot, snug in a dry sock, in.

↗ You can be very close to the end but a long way away. For this reason keep your nerve and focus until you cross the line because a lot can go wrong. And it often does.

The people I prefer are those who know they don't know. It's also a bit like the famous line from President George Bush (Jnr) when he talked about the 'known unknowns'.

Chapter 20
Life And Death

JIM IRWIN and his Filipino partner spent a lazy but stimulating four-hour lunch with myself and Nicola in Dublin's Shelbourne Hotel. He was a mentor and a man I looked up to as I mentioned in a previous chapter.

Three weeks later I learned he had committed suicide at his home in Florida. Only then did I realise that the lunch was his secret goodbye to us.

A careful, organised man, he knew what he was doing. He insisted there would be no funeral service. His death came as a total shock.

But it got me thinking — again — in terms of when the end comes.

Should we ask what it's all about?

Why do we climb mountains?

The more I travel this road and the more I learn, the more I learn that I don't know. The people I prefer are those who know they don't know. It's also a bit like the famous line from President George Bush (Jnr) when he talked about the 'known unknowns'.

Jim Irwin was an extraordinary man. An intense part of our last conversation, bordering on argument, was the core concept of infinity. He was wrestling to figure it out all his life. A simple enough word but the concept it represents has defied humanity in the same way as the concept of God. In trying to explain it, I think of trying to imagine what you cannot imagine. Could this be the concept of God itself?

I think this argument broke Jim. Not the one over our lunch in the Shelbourne; rather the bigger thought. There was no logic to explain it. And my guess is that, not helped by health issues, several marriages and complex problems with the US revenue, all had conspired to catch up. Death was his solution. He simply decided that was that and planned accordingly. American-born, he was proud of his Irish roots through his mum. He had become a multi-millionaire principally by selling ideas, his time and that of others through IMPAC.

For his British subsidiary, he had an English lord on his board of directors. He knew that opened doors to get business. It's not that he didn't like the English; he just hated class, snobbery and society's pecking order. As an Irish-American, he said he just liked having a lord on his payroll.

"The Brits make good servants and butlers," he joked. Perhaps.

I have a warmth for my Brit friends. I won't mention the name of one lord of the realm who was a bit stupid (but might sue my publisher). One time he fell asleep at an IMPAC business meeting; but he did open doors and create contacts, so he earned his keep, so to speak.

Jim took great delight in telling his story of being received by Queen Elizabeth II at her Balmoral abode in Scotland. He was presented with his Thai partner. She is a charming lady whom he had met at an ice-cream parlour where she worked. It started with a random conversation when Jim bought an ice-cream in Bangkok. Evidently he was out and about because the Thai 'hospitality' workers were on strike at the time.

"Oh! How charming, you and your lovely lady, where did you meet?" the Queen enquired. He outlined in a direct, honest way how they'd met — much to the shock of those in attendance.

"But the Queen found the conversation interesting," he told me.

Jim's success lay with cutting through the layers, keeping it simple and making it all into a process and then a focus.

Or to put it another way: in pre-television days, life was less cluttered. It used to be an 80:20 rule. People could understand and impact 80 percent of what was happening around them and 20 percent was out of their control. Now the situation has flipped 20:80 the other way. There is so much clutter and clatter out there in social media, immediacy, and instant access that it's organised chaos. Our attention spans are on a par with goldfish.

In my case, there was absolute focus to survive when circumnavigating. Without a mast, almost helpless, in one of the remotest parts of the world, there was little choice.

I was in instant satellite contact but it could take several days at best to be rescued. However, I remained in control, did not send a distress message and could eventually sail myself to safety.

More and more we watch life unfolding either on social media, radio or TV. We can do little. There is so much going on, with so many instant choices, it's almost impossible to decide what to do and what direction to take. Likewise we become more and more subject to group think and the computer. Algorithms are polarising us more as individuals. In a balanced society, people with extreme views are moderated by a spread in a community with checks and balances. Now however, the extremists — in whatever guise they may be — find themselves and find each other. They have their own networks, media channels and even their own language, and constantly reinforce and radicalise views. Much of the exercise is manipulated.

And how do we, in the middle of all this, make out as individuals and as a society? Dammed if I know.

The first big step is to understand what is happening. The polarisation, rules, control, extremes have fundamental principles similar to what George Orwell predicted. Only now they are in plain sight.

What does that mean for the rest of us?

I do know that in the middle of all the clutter you have to pick something (or a few things) and act. Focus and do what you do well. The rest of our lives starts NOW. It's simply impossible to do everything out there.

Life on the vast ocean, its scale and turbulence, calm and volatility make you realise how frail and insignificant we are.

For those reasons my philosophy on death is simple. Let's accept that we don't know.

In the interim, we must accept that some vast spiritual force is at play, outside our imagination. We must remain on the positive side of that force — and do the best we can.

Leadership

Leadership is living life to its fullest. In many ways it is about being a solutions provider. In my view, great leaders are those who spend their days finding and creating solutions. Leadership has many styles, be it from the front or behind. It's about focus and getting results. In essence we are all leaders and if you're smart you either lead, follow or get out of the way.

An example of leadership might be as mundane as how you might get a child to school because of a schedule change or having the boiler fixed. In my case it might have been dealing with broken equipment without any immediate apparent way to fix it deep in the Pacific Ocean.

Great leaders often emerge at a time of crisis.

The former Czech Republic president and writer, Vaclav Havel, came forward with a simple solution: "Get rid of the Communists and their way of control and thinking." The rest all fell into place. He led by being "politically incorrect' and by not conforming. And by not being afraid to confront, as so many others were at the time.

Lucie Bukova, the mother of my son Cormac, was a rebel and had strong links with the Havel family. As a result I was privileged to get an insight into this fascinating family and extraordinary period in history.

One day President Havel was in the hospital about to have one of his lungs removed (he was a smoker). Prior to being given the anaesthetic, he called the Czech government to the operating theatre. Each man smoked a cigarette and savoured the moment since it could have been the president's last — certainly for the lung that was destined for the scalpel.

It was this massive politically incorrect statement, the irony and black Czech humour that made Havel a leader. Yes, leaders break the norms and go against the grain.

Alone on my boat, I simply had no alternative but to find solutions to keep me safe and to finish the journey. There is a massive incentive if your life depends on it.

Many times something might break or come apart and I'd fail to solve the problem. Then it would get dark and no longer safe to work on deck. I'd sleep; I'd think about it. My mind would turn it over. And the following day, with a fresh start and a new approach, the problem would get solved.

Let me give you a practical example: The gooseneck is a fitting that connects the boom to the base of the mast.

It's a stainless steel swivel block that screws into the base of the boom. With a massive mainsail, strains on the boom are enormous. After dropping all sails and bearing off downwind, I struggled and failed for hours. Without this working I was in real trouble and there was no prospect of help.

All afternoon and evening I struggled. I tried many ways to reconnect the boom and mast. I gave up in desperation when it got dark. The following morning on first light I had a plan. It involved taking out the four sets of 'block-and-tackle' which had four-to-one mechanical advantage. They were otherwise used to secure the sails from moving around.

Then each "block-and-tackle" was strategically positioned to move the boom using leverage greater than my strength to move the boom end. Bit by bit I manoeuvred the end into place and reconnected it to the mast. Problem solved.

In work, I ask people to bring me their problems but only with their solutions. They may not be the right solutions but, at least, the thought process has started. If you are ever to prosper as a good leader it will be by being a good "solutions provider".

That is what leadership is about. It's also about knowing from who, what or where a solution can come.

Albert Einstein was emphatic when he said: "You don't ask the person to fix the problem who made the problem." I am not altogether sure about that. In my view, the most motivated fixer is the one who made the problem in the first place.

However, his point is likely to be that you need to constantly analyse problems from different perspectives; the same approach all the time will not bring a different result.

Love

This is a high-risk strategy to write about personally. I tread on delicate ground. I say that as a man who has been fortunate to have loved many and with a passion. Each day I wake up happy not to be thrown out. Indeed it was wonderful that, after a long time at sea and alone that my Lady Nicola, the love of my life of 12 years, took me back.

As a typical man, brought up in a sort of Catholic, Anglo-Saxon Celtic tradition, my emotions tend to be buried and not expressed.

As individuals, we are by definition solo. However, little happens in the universe without partnership, working together, pooling ideas and mutual support. In all my adventures, business and family life I have rarely been alone. I have had the good fortune to find, and work with, great partners.

Men and women need each other. When you throw raw emotion, passion and desire into the mix, logic goes out the window. I have had my share of turbulence and I have seen dark days when relationships ended and sparks flew. The reality of life is that sometimes couples grow together and other times they grow apart. This is fine. However, when you take the responsibility together to create human beings of the future and bring them into our universe, the dynamic changes.

And such is the beauty of it. Life is not a perfect picture and cannot be frozen in time. It is constant movement. A beautiful flower is not a moment in time. It seeds, grows, blooms, matures, withers and dies. A photograph is not a substitute for the real thing. Love, romance and the tension between the sexes bring a true spark to life.

In evolution, man was the hunter as he was physically stronger. The future will be different and it needs to be. Statistics show how women tend to be smarter, have more emotional maturity and work harder. The time of the "metro man" has come and attributes that kept him on top are fast disappearing.

For this reason society will be different. But we must stay close to nature, the environment, virtual reality and still maintain our freedoms.

Sometimes the most unlikely man hooks the most beautiful girl. He also can get a good boat and, to many people's surprise (including his own), create successful businesses and social enterprises. Like the Ying and the Yang, men and women are different. Also love and sex can get confused. They should not be mistaken for loyalty and commitment.

Anyway, you get my drift. In our internal personal lives of love and companionship, the rules of risk taking, living on the edge and pushing our boundaries also apply. If you don't ask, you don't get and you have to push yourself out there. And there is some truth in the old Irish proverb that "many women spend time spurning man's advances while later blocking their retreat".

Love, partnership, sex, desire, pleasure, companionship, fear of loneliness, adventure, exploration and most other things are all intertwined with human relationships.

And, when you disappear, like I have from time to time by going on my own across oceans for months at a time, you get to reflect a lot more on these matters.

Between work, play, service, eating, sleeping and all that consumes our time, we seldom get a chance to stand back from it all.

Why do we do what we do?

A fundamental question in life is: Why? Why do we do things? Why do we make decisions? And what are the great drivers to make things happen? Fear, though most are reluctant to admit, plays a major role in what we do and the decisions we take. It is directly linked with need. And all of this resonates with the issue of risk which I discussed at length earlier.

The evolution of Risk has had a similar story to Fear. We take risks out of fear as much as need. It's the mix of Need, Fear and Risk that drive and motivate.

Sadly Ireland has suffered from negative thinking. When Donald Trump visits us, he might localise his message with: "Let's Make Ireland Not-too-Bad Again."

How do we have this national characteristic? My theory is that we're small, we don't like to put our fellow equal citizens on pedestals because it says one is better than the other. We are not. We're all individuals, human beings, fundamentally the same. We live and eventually die. And what's more, we're all going to be a long time dead.

Another reason is our history. It is a sad one, filled with failure and tragedy. People are often obsessed by the past and failure, because success, winning and having no future — or so it may have seemed — made it that way.

Perhaps another reason is that we do not have the same affinity with the ocean. Historically most seafaring was associated with one-way traffic on the emigrant ship.

Even in 1916, when the Irish rebels were fighting to win freedom and dislodge our controlling neighbours, they forgot about the sea. They planned to take over the city centre and block all the roads — and did so. But they did not seek to block off the River Liffey, which runs from the Dublin mountains into the Bay and Irish Sea. In response, the British simply sailed their troop-laden gunboats up the Liffey and quickly won back control.

The point I'm making is that had the rebels tried to block the

Liffey they still might have failed, but they didn't even think about it. We were so well colonialised that it was not in the subconscious. And then, as if to add insult to injury, 100 years later on the 1916 anniversary celebrations, that historical fact was scarcely recognised.

Belfast is another good example. In recent times, a community obsessed by history spent vast sums on the Titanic Quarter.

Yet it has been a real struggle to sell investment in youth development through the Atlantic Youth Trust which has a mission to connect youth with the ocean and adventure.

Happily all of this negativity is changing, as is the expectation and celebration of failure, since success was rare.

¶ ¶ ¶ ¶

In a bizarre way, after achieving my sailing goal and dream, I can now set new horizons and get real joy, satisfaction and fulfilment in helping others achieve theirs.

While in the process I do not think I recognised it and certainly would never have admitted it. But my life was on hold and now I feel lucky to be starting the rest of it.

This is about goals, visions and horizons. Without these, little would happen.

¶ ¶ ¶ ¶

And while this book started 35,000 feet in the air on New Year's Day 2018, the story starts on New Year's Day 2016 and finishes on a New Year's Detox Atsumi retreat in Phuket, Thailand.

Each day this past week I've had a pipe up my interior pumping out the excess guff that accumulated over time. Also I have not eaten any food for more than seven days. And it's great.

I came here first more by accident than design for the first time 10 years ago. It was cold, lashing rain and miserable in traffic-jammed Dublin and I decided to fly early to Thailand and work online from there. My family was due there for Christmas and New Year later in the month anyway.

I checked in to the Atsumi Centre and to my horror found that each day started with colonics.

Basically you drink special compounds, you shove a pipe up your ass and each day your system — which accumulates so much junk — is pumped out. People, for example, may have enormous hard bellies but not be fat. Rather, undigested food and chemical substances that cannot be digested build up on the walls of our intestines. This build-up pushes out to make way for regular food. Even after a week, with no eating, it's amazing all the guff that keeps flowing out. Combined with amazing Thai massages, yoga, beach walks, lessons on diet and much more good stuff, I recommend it highly. Indeed we have made good friends with the owner Anna Khun and her extended family.

An amazingly powerful, petite 51-year-old, this lady embodies all the good about Thailand in her understanding and preparation of healthy foods, staying in shape, mothering three kids, giving work to six of her eight siblings (herself included) and work to brothers-in-law (even the divorced ones) and countless nieces and nephews. That's not to mention looking after her parents, ex-husband and current boyfriends. But you cross her at your peril.

Going back to basics and detox is a brilliant rejuvenation experience, stepping away from day-to-day pressures and responsibilities. Of course it also provided a clear head to finish writing this book. And God help the people when I get back to the office.

But Nicola will love it. From time to time we need to step out of day-to-day life, look hard at what's happening and think. Then you will be that small bit better from the experience. Life is about a constant reinvention, going forward, trying new things and doing your bit. The more you give the more you get.

Now it remains surreal to look back on it all, the highs and extreme lows on losing my mast in extreme conditions: the emotions, the drama, fear and bliss. It was a personal, terrifying, exciting voyage to the edge of life itself.

I hope you can benefit from my experiences, if not be amused by some of the adventures.

It has been 10 years since my last book 'The Unsinkable Entrpereneur' (it should have read "Unthinkable"). Now who knows what the next 10 years will bring?

Enjoy.

Thank you for sharing this journey. I look forward to your comments.

And I finish with the profound words of William Shakespeare:
'To be or not to be; that is the question.'

I mention again, for the last time, the secret to good navigation from an Irish friend: "Steer around the Rocks." It's back to basics really.

Keep it simple and stay lucky and alive — if you can.

LESSONS FROM CHAPTER 20

↗ If you're smart you either lead, follow or get out of the way.
↗ The more you give, the more you get.
↗ Don't give up.
↗ To succeed in Life, Leadership and Love the greatest fundamental you can build is trust — a fragile yet titanic word which is not unsinkable, yet is, unthinkable.
↗ Eternity, while a simple concept, is the most difficult, if not impossible, thing to understand.

In some respects it was like starting a new life with a blank canvas and becoming a born-again member of the human race (assuming we can call it human).

Epilogue
And Now For Something Completely Different

CROSSING the 'unofficial' finish line on April 1st, Easter Sunday 2018 brought closure to my solo circumnavigation. It was time to restart and move to new challenges and chapters.

That was it. Never again. From past lessons I know 'never' is a word we should never use. But that's it. Over.

In some respects it was like starting a new life with a blank canvas and becoming a born-again member of the human race (assuming we can call it human).

It was time to get back to work: the great adventures took much more of my savings than I will ever admit. It bordered on being selfish. I had spent several years spending my children's inheritance — before they might have taken the opportunity to lock me up.

And, while it perhaps only lay in my sub-conscious, I was looking for something new of a totally different kind. Sure, it was to make money, that's a given, but I had a real desire to make a difference. That difference was in addition to regular mainstays: looking after family and friends, climbing mountains such as Kilimanjaro and continuing with a life-long commitment to the Atlantic Youth Trust's mission to connect youth with the Ocean and Adventure.

Greg Gormley and Colm O'Reilly, who worked with me in Kilcullen Kapital, suggested we should buy the Sunday Business Post. Not just the newspaper on a Sunday — rather the actual business. I'm always up for a challenge and this was of a radically different kind. It was then a highly respected, national newspaper, which most agreed punched above its weight.

The paper was under threat. An independent media platform, it has a proud history. To boot it had talented journalists, production team and commercial people pulling it all together. In essence a really strong brand. With something like this, you don't take ownership, rather you get custody.

While others ran, I saw this as an opportunity. At the time, the paper business was the last thing on my mind when it presented itself. It could perhaps be compared with a turkey voting for Christmas. The perception was that it was something for a billionaire who wanted to be a millionaire to take on.

"A newspaper — you've got to be stone mad. It's an industry that is dying a death". That was a friend's reaction. He added: "You cannot say the business model is broken. If you say something is broken, you imply that it can be fixed. This is not the case."

Then I got further advice and, lo and behold, it was the same: "Stay away, don't touch it with a bargepole."

"You would be better off buying a building and collecting the rent", (another suggestion). And so on. If I wanted to gamble, Las Vegas was the best place to do so, I was told.

However, the more I looked at the opportunity, the more motivated and excited I became. Like all adventures there was a 'calculated risk' involved.

The challenge is on a par with setting out solo around the world — but this time bringing a team on the planned voyage. And what a voyage into our media's digital revolution. On the one part a commercial journey — reinventing what was considered as a sunset newspaper industry. On the other going with a band of journalists working harder, for less pay and not being understood. Individualistic by nature, they need to be not a part of the establishment.

Journalists and teachers are considered, in management terms, the most difficult to manage. And so it should be for tough leaders. Journalists need to be a little "outside" the so-called "establishment".

What attracted me most of all was the really loyal and dedicated team. They were all committed to business and the values of the Sunday Business Post. For some, it was their only job and they had worked in it since it was founded 30 years ago. Its alumni are a roll-call of the great and the good in Irish media, not just competing domestically but with our neighbours in the UK and further afield.

Besides being a business, its ownership was a social responsibility.

Clearly my motives were buying an undervalued business and making it buzz for a profit. However, the challenge went much deeper. Strong, independent and driven by fact are core values central to society. With such checks and balances, they are the foundations of democracy. Good journalism makes for transparency, disclosure and openness. It might seem "kitsch' trotting out such comments. However at my stage of existence on the final runway, sort to speak, I really had a desire to make a difference, to put something back in — and make the world a better place. I saw it as a real opportunity to focus skills learned over a lifetime, have some fun and make a profit in the process. I had also come to a stage in life that if I was to work, it was important to do so with something I'd enjoy, people I'd like, to make a real contribution. To do so it had to be profitable. Without that there would be no money to invest.

Profit is a term labelled as a bad word with the so-called left wing elite in Ireland. This is an island increasingly strangled by bureaucracy, with government's 'dead-hand' manifesting itself in every part of the economy. We suffer from what I term smoked-salmon socialism. Essentially unless business can make a profit, there will be nothing to tax, or funds for the state to look after those who can't help themselves or take on tasks that the private sector cannot or will not take on.

Clearly print has a future, but the business model has to change. A big part of the future for media — all agree — is digital across many platforms. You build communities and you interact with your consumer in a totally different way.

And so we decided to go for it. It's an understatement to call it a contrarian investment. We took on ownership of a highly respected brand and value system. The paper and team were fiercely proud of their independence and an important part of a functioning society that is seriously under threat in an area of declining advertising revenue bases and the switch to digital.

An act of serendipity might be another way to describe it. On a personal level it was a return to roots as an author and journalist. Several unrelated factors co-conspired.

In the process of building the picture, strategy, vision and plan whether correct or not, I was told there had been up to 34 suitors.

I took the time to talk with several of those in Ireland, the UK and the US who had expressed an interest in the publication. Gradually we built up a picture of why they were interested and why they never did the deal.

In effect we were the "last man standing" and while a confidential process, at this point it was an open secret for months that the business was for sale.

More by accident than design I had come in at the end of the sale process. Perhaps frustrated by the failure of a new IT system or management challenges or personality issues (I don't know) Key Capital the owners decided they wanted out. The IT system was from a South African firm and there seemed to have been a disconnection in scoping it out and implementing it. I don't know what went wrong here and I am not qualified to comment. However, I do know that internal buy-in for change is critical. I refer you to our three-step process below.

Of course it's human nature for people working in set ways to be all for change. However for the love of God do not ask them to do anything different.

I guess the failure of this investment to go forward (in fairness they got most of their money back) could be singled out as an example of culture eating strategy for breakfast.

In fact they had a trade buyer — not the Irish Times (a then-obvious purchaser) who had expressed interest in buying. But to get a good market price and find a good new owner they decided to put it on the market through a corporate finance house in a private and confidential process.

But in media, the reality is that very little is confidential. The fact the business was on the market quickly became an open secret.

It was a logical buy for the Irish Times in that they had a daily paper, six days a week, but no Sunday. Instead they bought the Irish Examiner — a competing daily paper with its roots in Cork and Munster. This to me, other than perhaps printing and production synergies, is devoid of logic.

It is in all our interests for the Examiner to thrive and prosper. However in a declining market, I would be concerned it could pull down The Irish Times, a paper of record and important fabric of Irish society.

The other trade buyer then decided not to get involved in an auction process.

From research on the ground we were being told that, despite being a business paper, much of its tone and comment had become 'anti-business', almost socialist in outlook.

My view is that while they were doing a great job, the publication had become too political, and perhaps disconnected from the real frontline of business.

No matter what was said about it, the Post was clearly punching above its weight. It's not for a publisher to dictate what journalists and editors should cover. However, there are boundaries.

Like many other nationalities, we suffer from Group Think from time to time. What happened with the banks or the state's relationship with the church are cases in point. These are views strongly held by Ray Bassett, former diplomat and highly-regarded Post columnist.

I revert to my fundamental belief that business must make profit — and to do so is about looking after people — they are not polar opposites. A business has to be successful for people to be motivated for a return on effort. Without success there can be no creation of wealth and without this nothing to tax for society to divide or provide services.

I also believe strongly that openness and transparency are hallmarks of the future in every way.

Without being disrespectful to those who went before, on buying the Business Post one got the feeling the culture of the paper was 'anti-business'.

And that's my basis of thinking for the sort of guidelines determined for the business. In fact Donald Trump has done a big favour to quality journalism. In his simple mind he has linked social media reports on the likes of Twitter, Facebook and so forth with well-balanced fact-checked media articles from trusted brands.

He has branded it all 'fake news'. Essentially he had two categories to attack: One with facts, content or views with which he did not agree, and wrong information. The irony is that he speaks so many untruths he is one of the largest retailers of fake news.

Increasingly society is becoming more and more polarised as we see through the internet. Through machine-driven computer algorithms I refer to elsewhere in this book people are being fed 'facts' that confirm their views — whatever they may be — pushing elements of society further and further apart. At the extreme, it's the way Trump and his supporters target journalists and media who challenge their views. That is history repeating itself in how fascism developed in Germany in the 1930s. Trump winding up people's fears about immigration so he can build his wall with Mexico, is like the McCarthy frenzy in the Fifties. History repeats itself in odd ways

To put it another way, those at the edge or extremes are finding each other, helped by technology. They move more and more to the edge. The great irony is it is happening in plain sight. The massive manipulation of social media in the US elections is clear. The irony is that such was its success that many do not realise it was, and is being, done to them.

It's alarming the way society is going. When leaders start creating justifications for chopping the fingers off people before killing them; when dissident journalists disappear — as in the case of Jamal Khashoggi — we have problems. Jamal was murdered for speaking out.

Back in the newspaper, in our challenge to reinvent the enterprise, actual change management is a challenging business. In approaching the Business Post, or any other business or enterprise, the fundamentals are the same — though people will argue: "but this is a different situation". The fundamental principle of business, and indeed life, does not change. I learned that from Jim Irwin, whom I mentioned earlier. "The principles apply across cultures and countries," Jim often said.

Granted a business that sells newspapers is different from one that sells cosmetics. But peel back the layers and the fundamentals are the same. And with the Business Post we had the added twist that independent media and thought leadership are fundamental building blocks of society in an age of "group think".

We broke down change for the Business Post, as in other businesses, into three stages.

Christ was the best communicator of all when he explained the three concepts: The Father, The Son and the Holy Ghost.

Barack Obama, also a great communicator, always spoke three concepts at a time.

In this process we were fortunate in securing the consultancy services of Aileen O'Toole. Aileen was one of the original founders and remains highly respected in Irish media; she has reinvented herself as a digital specialist.

Brian MacNeice, of Kintos strategy consultants also came on board supported by Colm O'Reilly of Kilcullen. The final member of the change team is Declan Dooley, whom we were fortunate to get during his career transition from running and owning both the Cork and Galway Independent newspapers. Then, from over the horizon, came Odran Ginnity for the technology architecture, who has read the situation very well.

▶ The First Stage in change, as in the Business Post, was to establish the current situation with all the team in an organisation. While as an external force coming in it may have been obvious, if you want or need to bring change, for survival, those who you want to change must understand what is wrong. This involved a confidential, detailed staff survey, to which 80% responded. No surprise, the results were very negative but the comments were invaluable.

▶ The Second Stage is to scope out exactly what needs to be done. This relates to establishing a strategy, the resources necessary and what is achievable and what is not. It is also to set goals and objectives and identify where everybody wants to be. Clearly in media the strategy is especially challenging in the need to create a new business model.

▶ The Third Stage is implementation and establishing KPIs — key performance indicators — and evaluating. In particular in our new digital age, everything we have learned is about measurement. This in particular was driven home from the Jeff Bezo's approach in reinventing the Washington Post as a software company.

And in building the model we have looked around the world for best practice, including an informative trip to the Washington Post and Business Media in Scandinavia. In the quest for a dynamic new business model for the Post there is not much point in reinventing the wheel; rather to take the best of what is there to enhance our own and build a world class business.

As this book takes shape, so too is the Business Post challenge under way. There is no quick fix. However, we are applying my fundamental 'Three rules of Change Management' above and all our team are hopeful of success. From a personal perspective, there is no question of not succeeding.

It will take time, and to date the Business Post ranks as a great fascinating Journey.... to the Edge. Let's see.

Like life itself, eventually it all comes to an end. Or does it? An early mentor and a man I admire, Tim Pat Coogan, so called his home 'Eventually' — a profound name.

The word is important in our existence but is subservient to the concept of infinity I discussed earlier as the most difficult, if not impossible, concept to understand.

And this with the concept of Risk, a fundamental of mankind's journey to the Edge and perhaps beyond the black hole is my shared take-away from this narrative; I've explored it earlier in how its abuse through control and technology could kill our civilisation.

And, on three more life stages of life on this journey, I have had:

1st — Youth.

2nd — I am still voyaging through eternal middle age and ready.

3rd — And heading to the final stage: "Sure you're looking well."

As in life itself, we always strive for perfection but never seem to get there. But now in the end, I have reached perfection.

And that means that finally I have become the Perfect Eejit.

In life it's important to take what we do seriously, leave something for the other guy, put something back in and never to take ourselves seriously, seriously!?

And Finally ...

Either way, lead, follow or get out of the way. I sincerely hope that with my commitment to media with the Business Post and other enterprises under Kilcullen Kapital Partners I can make a difference.

Likewise the maritime has been good to me. It is a reason why I renewed my commitment to the Atlantic Youth Trust Charity in connecting youth with ocean and adventure and my aspiration to 'put something back in'. Friendships are important, as is the belief that we are not alone in the world. Many have helped on the way, for this I am in debt and appreciative. There is a spirit, an extra force, a God; but it's something that cannot be imagined and contrasts positive and negative, good and evil.

Never forget the importance of knowing there is a lot you simply don't know. For me, understanding the concept of eternity and infinity is the greatest conundrum of them all. And watch out for the Black Holes.

Thanks for sharing my journey. I hope we have learned some lessons.

Who knows what's next over the Edge?

Let's see. I look forward. Thanks.

FINAL LESSONS LEARNED
- There are no secrets in media, nor should there be; independent journalism is a fundamental part of a free democratic society.
- Most people want to change — but don't ask them to do anything different.
- The most important thing in change is to bring people with you and make it a 'Win-Win'.
- Great communication comes in threes. Keep the message simple (a bit like Irish jokes so that our English friends can understand them.)
- Just Do It.
- We'll all be a long time dead.

Appendix

A brief explanation of some terms

Aft quarter: The rear part of the vessel.

Battens: 'Stiffeners' to maintain the shape of sails. They often run the full length of the mainsail and need to be light, strong and flexible. They are generally made from carbon fibre

Blast Reacher: A special sail used for reaching, or going with the wind at an angle for around 90 degrees (on the side). Used in strong winds.

Block and tackle: A 'block' is a pulley. 'Tackle' is another term for rope or lines. Joined together the terms usually mean a combination of both for mechanical advantage.

Boom gooseneck: The boom is the pole coming from the mast as a bottom base for the mainsail. The gooseneck is the point where the boom is connected to the mainsail.

Bow: The front end of a boat.

Cantered keel: A keel which can be moved and adjusted for stability.

Hydro generator: A special generator that generates electricity from the power of the ocean.

Furling line: A line that usually goes from the cockpit of the boat, forward to assist in the 'furling' or rolling of the sail.

Gybe: This is when you are sailing downwind and altering course where the boom is moved from one side of the boat to the other

J1 J2, J3 etc Sails: These are headsails or sails that are set on the front of the boat before the mast. And like changing gears on a car you change sails for different conditions and wind speeds. A J1 is a bigger sail for lighter winds from 5 to 10 knots approx; a J2

from 10 to 20 knots, a J3 from 20 knots to 35 knots (storm force)

Halyard: The rope used to hoist the sails. For the smaller sails the Halyard is generally lower down.

Jib: a triangular staysail set forward of the mast

Jury rig: The jury rig is an emergency or temporary sail and mast.

Jury rig port: A base where the jury rig is mounted.

Keel: This is on the bottom of the boat and gives stability. On the IMPCO Vendée boat it is usually more than four metres deep

Lazy Jacks: Special ropes coming from the mast that holds the boom up when the mainsail is not set. When the mainsail is set the Jacks, or lines, are no longer needed — hence the term 'lazy'.

Runner: The line that holds up the mast from the stern or the back of the boat.

Weather Runner: There are usually two Runners. The Weather is the one on the side from which the wind is blowing.

Reef line: The reef line is a rope that is used to shorten sail or to reduce the sail area when the wind is strong.

Reef clew lines: These are the reef lines attached to the clews which is the back part of the sail.

Spinnaker: A large sail, like a parachute, which is flown when the wind is astern or coming from behind.

Spars: A general term for masts or other rigging.

Starboard: The right-hand side of the boat facing forward.

The Main: Generally an abbreviation for the mainsail. It is the largest sail behind the mast.

Acknowledgements

WHILE this was a 'solo' navigation, I found out quickly that we are never alone. The title of this book *Journey to the Edge* — is on one hand an account of my time at seas but also a metaphor for life itself. In an odd way, going it alone has made me realise the value of friendship, human company and the fact that in humanity we all need each other. It was said centuries ago with the statement that: "No man is an island…"

Firstly, I want to thank my wife 'The Lady Nicola' for taking me back after being alone at sea for so long. I also want to signal my gratitude to my family, brothers, sisters, cousins and in particular my own children Cormac, Saoirse, Aisling and Roisin. And then Nicola's spirited bunch, Louis, Anna and Joe… And in the true "Modern Family" spirit an acknowledgement for Lucie Patrick, Suzanna and, of course, Toby.

I would like to record by deep appreciation to all who made the journey possible. To Marcus Hutchinson, my project manager, for his understanding and Roger Courtney at office HQ, holding it all together with Richard Klecka, Neil O'Hagan and many others, such as John Killeen, who helped — some more than others — and some not realising it at all, at all.

A special thanks to President Michael D. Higgins and team members, Claire Power and Kevin McCarthy.

And then making this book, the brothers Cunningham, Eddie and PJ, a great editing team. Also to Joe Coyle for his design work and laying the photos and text out for maximum effect. To Peter Kelly who managed to make sense of all the oddball video footage for a film of the adventure.

Listed below, I wish to acknowledge as many as possible and give them all a mighty 'shout-out' — and in particular to those not included, 'twas not possible to list everyone as the printer's deadline loomed — or you may be lucky?

Delia Alinas, Peter Allen, Roisin Armstrong, Wesley Armstrong, Hugh Bailey, Andrew Baker, Scott Baker, Peter Bastable, David Beattie, David Becvar, Frederique Bedos, Gerry Bell, Charlie Bergen, Russell Best, Jamie Boag, Herve Borde, Peter Bowring, Annmarie Bowring, Ivana Bozdichova, Richard Branson, Gerry Brennan, Radek Brnak, Marian Broderick, Paul Brosnan, Michael Brown, Kristina Bukova, Lucie Bukova, Anjeliqoy Buoy, Roman Buoy, Francois Buoy, Maxime Buoy, Mary Burke Kennedy, Des Burke Kennedy, Alan Burnside, Rebecca Burrell, Killian Bushe, Derek Butler, Geraldine Byrne Nason.

Daniel Calero, Jose Juan Calero, Pepe Calero, Jacques Caraes, Anne Chambers, Andrew Collins, Roger Conan, John Concannon, Eamon Conneely, Peter Cooke, Stephen Cooney, Michael Cotter, Roger Courtney, Simon Coveney, John Coyle, James Coyle, Chris Craig, Harry Cudmore, Sean Cullen, Bill Cullen, Tony Cummins, Conor Daly, Amanda Davis, Conchur DeBarra, Ger Dempsey, Thomas Denmark, Honza Denmark, Sylvian Derreumaux, Dermot Desmond, Hugues Destremeau, Robert Dix, Brian Dobson, Declan Dolan, Peter Donnolly, John Donnolly, Declan Dooley, William Dowering, Jerry Dowling, Jimmy Dowling, Tom Doyle, Richard Duggan, Christian Dumard, Zbynek Dvorak.

Rob Eliott, Guillaume Evrard, Vladimir Ezr, Jim Fahy, Brian Fallon, Chuck Feeney, Stephen Fisher, Tom Fitzpatrick, John Flaherty, Dave Flynn, Conal Forbes, Cyril Forbes, George Formandl, Frabazio Fraboni, Cathal Friel, Carlo Gherardi, Ewan Gibb, Mark Gibney, Michael Gill, Eamon Gilmore, Greg Gormley, Karel Gott, Albert Grimaldi, Tim Gunning, Frantsiek Hala, Alastair Hammond, Stefan Hansen, Frank Haughton, Frank Heath, Colm Hendrick, Pat Hernon, Pieter Herrema, Aidan Higgins, Robin Hogg, Ron Holland, Stewart Hosford, Larry Howell, Susi Huber, Ashley

Huber, Marcus Hutchinson, Meagan Hutchinson, Tim Huurman, Mairead Huurman, Johan Huurman, Mary Hynes.

Jaroslav Jirman, Noel Johnstone, Fiona Johnstone, Kaisa Kado, Daniela Kafkova, Michael Kane, Billy Kane, Gary Keane, Des Kelleher, Enda Kelly, Peter Kelly, David Kenefick, Neil Kenefick, Declan Kennedy, Enda Kenny, Sean Keogh, Richard Klecka, Brid Korby, Nick Koumarianos, Ales Kratochvíl, Josef Krepinsky, Katka Krizek, Petr Kucera, Roger Lacey, Ruairi Lannen, Gerard Lawless, Billy Lawless, Dean Lawrence, Ruth Lemass, Sean Lemass, Sylvie Lepoutre, Andrea Leprisova, Daniela Liebing, Hana Lilanová, Andrea Linehan, Steve Little, Brian Lynch.

Anna Mackey, Vibjorn, Madsen, Olga Magliocco, Tangi Mahe, Gildas Mahé, Liavan Mallin, Nigel Mansley, Catherine Maybury, Trevor McClintock, Daniel McCloskey, James McCollum, John McDonald, Cormac McDonnacha, Mona McDonnell, Martin McDonnell, Tina McKenzie, Stuart McLachlan, Niamh McMahon, Jimmy McShane, Sean McVeigh, Hendrick Melle, Sean Melly, Mary Menton, Paul Mitchell, Ian Mitchell, Nicola Mitchell, Gay Mitchell, Kevin Moore, Viki Moore, Pauline Moran, Ken Moran, Maria Moynihan Lee, Helen Mulcahy, Michael Mullen, Elizabeth Mullen, Tony Mullet, Joan Mulloy, Niall Mulqueen, Joanne Murphy, Sarah Murphy, Caroline Murphy, Dirk Nauta, Robert Nemec, Sarah Newman, Winkie Nixon, Chris Nolan, Catherine Noone, Davie Norris, Peter Novotny.

Pádraig Ó Ceidigh, Micheál Ó hAmhláin, Cormac Ó hAmhláin, David O'Brien, Michael O'Brien, Suzanna O'Coineen, Cormac B O'Coineen, Roisin O'Coineen, Aisling O'Coineen, Saoirse O'Coineen, Ian O'Connell, Niamh O'Connor, Paddy O'Connor, Rory O'Donnellan, Neil O'Dowd, Len O'Hagan, Neil O'Hagan, Gerard O'Hare, Nicholas O'Leary, Owen O'Malley, Martin O'Malley, Marie O'Neill, Colm O'Reilly, Tony O'Reilly, Sean O'Rourke, Donal O'Shaughnessey, Padraig O'Tuairisc, Mairead O'Tuairisc.

Dave Parker, Ged Pierce, Shelia Pimm, Michal Pozar, Pierce Purcell, Pierce Purcell Jnr, Dag Pyke, Averyl Quinn, Cormac Rabbitt, John Rabbitt, Eoin Rabbitt, Nima Ramezanopour, Harpal Randhawa, Jiri Rasner, Jana Ridanova, Fred Robin, Tom Roche, Ken Rogers, Tracy Rohan, Patrick Ronaldson, Anna Ronaldson, Louis Ronaldson, Joe Ronaldson, Barbora Roubalova, Adrian Rowan, Pavel Rozsypal, Thomas Ruyant, Declan Ryan, Rob Shesol, Vladimir Skolout, Eva Skorepova, Zdenek Sluka, Ian Smith, Johnny Smullen, Bernard Sommers, Martin Stachník, Jack Stack, Jana Stastny, Dermot Stokes, Zdenek Stuchlik, Maria Surboeck, Hana Svehlackova, Mel Symes.

Klaus Tebbe, Tony Tennyson-Pierre, Antoine Tesson, Christophe Thillez, Phillipe Thomas, Alex Thomson, John Toner, John Treacy, Stephen Treacy, Simon Troel, Ryan Tubridy, Jan Urbanm Andrew Vaughan, Ajit Virk, Ian Walker, John Walsh, Rodney Walshe, Billy Walshe, Michael White, Jonathan Wilkinson, Shane Woodroffe, Shane Young and Jamie Young.

Index